Sports Nutrition for Teenagers

Author: Jacob Nelson, B.S. Exercise Science, NASM, ACSM-EP

Editor: Mary Dieterich

Proofreaders: Alexis Fey and April Hawkins

COPYRIGHT © Mark Twain Media, Inc.

ISBN 978-1-62223-920-7

Printing No. CD-405099

Mark Twain Media, Inc., Publishers
Distributed by Carson Dellosa Education

The purchase of this book entitles the buyer to reproduce the student pages for classroom use only. Other permissions may be obtained by writing Mark Twain Media, Inc., Publishers.

All rights reserved. Printed in the United States of America.

Visit us at www.marktwainpublishing.com

Table of Contents

Unit I. Introduction to Sports Nutrition

Sports Nutrition for Teenagers is designed to teach students and athletes the fundamentals of nutrition as well as how to use those nutrition principles to improve their sports performance on and off the field. The human body may be the most versatile machine on this earth. Through years of practice, most people can be proficient in just about any sport they'd like to play. You might not become good enough to play in the NBA, but most people can still learn how to play basketball, given enough time and effort. Through time, effort, and practice, humans are capable of reaching incredible feats of athleticism.

Thinking of our bodies as machines, all machines require the right fuel in order to perform their tasks and duties. Historically, most cars have required gasoline to propel themselves forward on the highway. New technology has made it possible for vehicles to also run on battery power and potentially even water someday. Much like cars, humans require fuel to produce the energy to perform our tasks (in the case of this book, movement during sports). This book hopes to teach what type of fuel your body will need to perform the best in your sport. Humans are designed with three different types of energy systems that all use different types of energy depending on the type of activity. Swinging a baseball bat once uses a very different kind of energy system and thus needs different food than someone running a marathon. One utilizes the creatine phosphate energy system while the other relies on the oxidative, or aerobic, energy system for fuel. Not only do different sports require different types of fuel, but the body is constantly producing different byproducts, like sweat, that we have to manage during our sports so that we don't become dehydrated, cramp, and suffer in our performance.

If you are a sumo wrestler, your goal will be to gain as much weight as you can, even if it is fat, to improve your performance. If you are a ballet dancer, it might be a huge advantage to stay as light as you can so that you can jump and dance easier without putting too much stress on your joints. If you are a wrestler, you might have to quickly cut weight to make your team's weight class. If you're a linebacker, you might want to gain as much muscle as you can while keeping any body fat gain to a minimum so you can keep your speed on the field but also tackle as hard as you can. If you're sweating on the soccer field during a double header on a hot 80-degree day, you might be fighting off dehydration headaches and muscle cramps that could end your soccer career if your muscles tear while cramping.

The goal of this book is to empower athletes to manage any and all obstacles that might come their way in the process of fueling their bodies to perform the best they possibly can for their sport. In order to do this, this book will cover the foundations of nutrition so that athletes have a general understanding of nutrition and how it impacts the body. They will learn about macronutrients so that they can better understand how to safely lose and gain weight depending on their sport needs. They will also learn about micronutrients and their role in staying healthy and recovering from strenuous workouts. Athletes will learn how to manage their hydration levels, including their electrolytes, to keep performance high when it matters most. The basic guidelines on supplementation will be covered to give athletes the biggest edge in their sport while staying safe and optimizing their health as well as their performance.

Unit II. Nutrition Fundamentals

Nutrition Overview

Nutrition can be defined as the study of how food affects the human body and all its processes. This includes digestion and how the body uses the nutrients after digesting, specifically during sports performance. Food is the fuel that our bodies break down and convert into useful energy. The components of food can be broken down into calories, carbohydrates, proteins, fats, vitamins, minerals, and fiber. Proper sports nutrition is crucial to help teenage athletes continue to grow, not only improving their physical health but also maintaining their mental health and preventing chronic fatigue and sickness.

Calories

Calories are a unit of measurement that tells us how much energy is in the food we eat. Technically, one calorie is the amount of energy needed to raise the temperature of 1 gram of water by 1 degree Celsius. In nutrition, calories are used to quantify the amount of energy our body gets when consuming food and beverages to use during functions like breathing, moving, and fueling physical activity. Calories can be used immediately after consumption or they can be stored as either glycogen or adipose tissue in the body. **Glycogen** is stored carbohydrates, or sugar, inside the body that you can readily use as quick access energy for intense activities. They are stored in the liver and in the muscles. Keeping your glycogen stores topped up during exercise is one of the keys to optimal performance that we will discuss later in this book. **Adipose tissue**, or body fat, is a specialized type of cell that stores energy in the form of lipid, or body fat, beneath the surface of the skin (**subcutaneous fat**) and around internal organs (**visceral fat**). Body fat, or adipose tissue, can be thought of as long-term fuel storage. Unlike glycogen, which provides quick energy for sports, body fat is best used during prolonged activity, like running a 10k or a marathon, when food isn't readily available. This is basically endurance training.

At rest, a 100-pound person burns anywhere from 40–50 calories per hour, adding up to 960–1,200 calories per day. This is called their **Basal Metabolic Rate (BMR)**. It takes calories, or energy, to do basic things like breathing, pumping the blood in your body through circulation, and maintaining body temperature. The more you weigh, the more calories you burn at rest. This is also influenced by how much muscle mass you have. Every pound of muscle burns an additional 10–20 extra calories per day. If a 100-pound person exercises and gains 20 pounds of muscle, they would burn an additional 200–400 calories (20 x 10 = 200, 20 x 20 = 400) per day at rest. This would put their resting metabolic rate between 1,160–1,600 calories per day. Gaining muscle drastically increases the amount of calories someone needs per day.

Humans are always burning calories, even if they aren't moving or doing anything because it requires energy to simply stay alive and keep up with normal bodily functions. Since movement also requires energy, the more you move, the more calories, or fuel, you need to continue movement and to stay alive. Let's take a Poptart®, my favorite snack when I was a teenager. There are about 400 calories in a package of Poptarts®. If I weigh 100 pounds, that Poptart® is going to contain enough fuel to last me about one-third to one-half of the day if my calorie needs

Unit II. Nutrition Fundamentals (cont.)

are only 960–1,200. I will use those calories from the Poptart® my entire morning. The more I move, the faster I burn up those calories. What happens if I run out of calories before lunch? If we didn't have storage units within our body (glycogen and body fat), I would drop dead when I ran out of fuel, exactly the same as a mower stops when it runs out of gasoline to burn. Luckily, we aren't mowers and we have a couple thousand calories stored as glycogen in our liver and in our muscles, and then after using that energy reserve, we have thousands, sometimes hundreds of thousands, of calories in our body fat that my body can tap into once the Poptarts® are burnt up. I will use these energy reserves while my body sends hunger signals, called **ghrelin**, to my brain telling me it's time to eat. Ghrelin is the hormone responsible for telling your brain "Eat now!!!" and is why you feel ravenous before you eat. Once you start eating, your body produces less ghrelin and more **leptin**, which is the hormone responsible for telling you you've had enough to eat and you can stop eating now.

As you can see, hunger is driven by signals, called **hormones**, that help us know when our fuel is running out (ghrelin) and when we are fueled enough for the next few hours of activity (leptin). When we eat, we use up those calories during the next few hours of life. If we eat more than we could possibly burn, say all-you-can-eat buffet-style, our bodies will store the extra calories as either glycogen or body fat so that we can use it later down the road. While basal metabolic rate is important to get a baseline of our calorie needs to just stay alive, as athletes, we know we are doing much more than staying alive. We're constantly on the run and burning energy in practice, games, and all of our activities throughout the regular school day. For the purposes of this book, think of your basal metabolic rate as your baseline energy requirements for that day. It is not advisable to eat below your baseline, even if you are trying to lose weight. It is very easy to damage your metabolism if you try eating much less than your basal metabolic rate for any period of time. This can lead to eating disorders, crash dieting, loss of muscle mass, loss of performance, and a huge dip in overall health. You should almost never eat below your basal metabolic rate, but rather use your daily tasks and exercise as your method for weight loss. By adding in your daily activities to your basal metabolic rate, you will get your Total Daily Energy Expenditure.

Total Daily Energy Expenditure (TDEE)

Total Daily Energy Expenditure (TDEE) is how many calories you burn per day at rest and throughout all your daily activities. This is important for athletes to understand so that they can manage how many calories they need to ingest per day to stay the same weight or if they need to gain (**positive energy balance**) or lose (**negative energy balance**) weight. Calculating your TDEE can be done easily using the **Weight-Based Rule of Thumb method** explained on the following page. There are more complicated formulas, such as the Harris-Benedict equation, that give more accurate caloric needs, but for the introductory level of this book, we will use the easiest formula. Many of these calculators can be found online by searching for TDEE formulas that will ask about height, weight, and daily activity to give you a more accurate number so you don't have to do the calculations yourself.

Unit II. Nutrition Fundamentals (cont.)

The Weight-Based Rule of Thumb Formula:

Daily Calorie Needs = Body Weight (in pounds) X Activity Factor

- Activity Factors (calories per pound)
  - Low Activity (minimal exercise, mostly resting): 12–14 calories/pound
  - Moderate Activity (sports 3–5 days/week, school activities): 15–17 calories/pound
  - High Activity (intense sports daily, very active): 18–22 calories/pound

Example:

- A 130-pound soccer player (moderate activity, practices 4 days/week):
  - 130 x 15–17 = 1,950–2,210 calories per day
- A 90-pound gymnast (high activity, daily training):
  - 90 x 18–22 = 1,620–1,980 calories per day
- A 200-pound football player off-season (minimal exercise, mostly resting):
  - 200 x 12–14 = 2,400–2,800 calories per day
- A 200-pound football player in pre-season (lifting or conditioning every day, very active):
  - 200 x 18–22 = 3,600–4,400 calories per day

Name: ______________________________ Date: ____________________

Unit II. Nutrition Fundamentals (cont.)

Activity 1: Practice the Weight-Based Rule of Thumb equation given the scenario in the table below.

Complete the table, My Monthly Calorie Needs, using the example of a 130-pound summer softball and winter basketball player.

My Monthly Calorie Needs				
Month	**My Weight**	**My Activity Level**	**Calorie Range (Weight x Activity Factor)**	**My Daily Calorie Needs (Average Calories/Day)**
January	130	High (basketball, 6x per week)	130 x 18–22 = 2,340–2,860	(2,340 + 2,860)/2 = ~2,600
February	128	High (basketball, 6x per week)		
March	132	Moderate (basketball, 4x per week)		
April	133	Low (off-season, no practice)	133 x 12–14 = 1,596–1,862	
May	135	Moderate (softball, 4x per week)		
June	135	High (softball, 6x per week)		
July	137	High (softball, 6x per week		
August	138	Moderate (softball, 4x per week)		
September	136	Low (off-season, no practice)		
October	138	Moderate (working part time retail, 4 x week)		
November	141	Moderate (working part time retail, 4x per week)		
December	141	High (basketball, 4x per week plus retail, 3x per week)	141 x 18–22 = 2,538–3,102	(2,538 + 3,102)/2 = ~2,820

Name: ______________________ Date: ______________

Unit II. Nutrition Fundamentals (cont.)

Activity 2: Now, create and calculate your own calorie needs for the next 30 days based on the Weight-Based Rule of Thumb equation and how often you think you will be practicing or performing your sport. Think of off-season weight training, in-season performance, or if you're currently not doing anything and in the off-season, your own activity level based on your hobbies or activities. Take into consideration part-time jobs (if they're active or sedentary) and your own hobbies (whether you enjoy playing video games in your down time or prefer to spend time biking or doing physically demanding activities). The more you move, the higher on the equation list you'll be. If you aren't very active and prefer low-stress relaxation like movies or tv shows, the lower on the equation you'll be.

My Monthly Calorie Needs				
Month	**My Weight**	**My Activity Level**	**Calorie Range (Weight x Activity Factor)**	**My Daily Calorie Needs (Average Calories/Day)**

Activity 3: As you can see, calorie needs vary depending on how much you weigh and how much you exercise. Smaller people need fewer calories and larger people need more calories to sustain weight and provide enough energy for optimal performance. What makes matters even more complicated is that during pre-season or regular season, your calories may be drastically higher than during the off-season when you're letting your body rest. If you don't take an off-season, your calorie needs may be high all year long. For this reason, it's important to understand and do your calorie needs calculation monthly.

Thanks to puberty, your weight will change monthly simply from growing into your adult body. Your activity also changes monthly based on what sports you have going on that month. Even if you eat exactly what you think you will burn, you are also likely still growing through puberty and your weight will either increase or decrease naturally as you get taller and grow. For this reason, make a habit of calculating your calorie needs monthly to give you a rough estimate of how much you need to eat that month. This will help fuel your current performance as well as help you lose or gain weight later on depending on your sport.

The table on page 7 can help keep track of your own daily needs over the next year.

Name: ______________________________ Date: ____________________

Unit II. Nutrition Fundamentals (cont.)

My Monthly Calorie Needs				
Month	**My Weight**	**My Activity Level**	**Calorie Range (Weight x Activity Factor)**	**My Daily Calorie Needs (Average Calories/Day)**
January				
February				
March				
April				
May				
June				
July				
August				
September				
October				
November				
December				

Unit III. Macronutrients Overview

Macronutrients Overview

In the last chapter, we talked about how all food can be broken down into energy as fuel for the body. That energy is called calories and will keep your body alive and will also fuel your workouts, games, and all your daily activities. Calories can be further broken down into macronutrients. **Macronutrients** are the essential nutrients found in food that are required by the human body in large quantities to sustain life, provide energy, and support growth and development. There are three macronutrients: proteins, carbohydrates, and fats. **Calories can be broken down into grams of each macronutrient. 1 gram of protein contains exactly 4 calories. 1 gram of carbohydrates also contains 4 calories. 1 gram of fat contains 9 calories.** This is why the back of a food label will tell you how many calories per serving and how much protein, carbohydrates, and fats in grams that food has. This chapter will discuss all of the macronutrients and explain the importance of each in terms of sports nutrition.

Protein Overview

Protein is often referred to as the building blocks of life. To fully understand protein, think of our bodies as one giant Lego® city. The city is always growing, fixing worn down buildings, and building new buildings. In this city, proteins are like the castles, buildings, houses, skyscrapers, and even your local YMCA. Most people hear the word *protein* and immediately think of muscles, but protein is much more than that. Just like all of the infrastructure, or buildings, in our city, protein makes up all of our organs including our heart, lungs, skin, fingernails, hair, muscle mass, tendons, ligaments, and so much more. You see, each building made up of a ton of building blocks neatly put together to perform its job is similar to each organ being put together by different types of protein to perform its job in the body. Protein can be broken down one more time into amino acids.

Amino acids are like the individual Lego® blocks that you can piece together into making the larger protein structure. When we eat food containing protein, typically thought of as our meat (which actually includes all meat, fish, eggs, dairy, beans, and soy), our stomach breaks down the food into amino acids. From there, we can use the amino acids to build muscle, aid in our immune function, recover and heal from energy use, and for brain development and function.

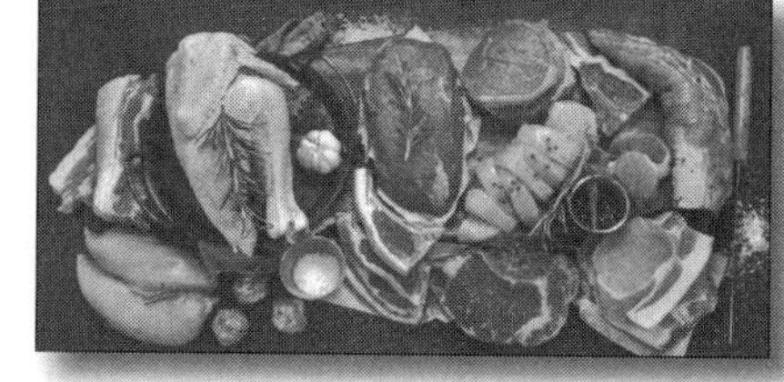

Our bodies require 20 different types of amino acids. Think of 20 different-colored or shaped building blocks. Our bodies are incredibly efficient because through different combinations of those 20 types of blocks, they can build all of the many types of buildings in our "cities"—our organs, enzymes, muscles, skin, hair, tendons, and ligaments. Different amino acids have different tasks in the body that we will discuss in later chapters. For now, know that there are 11 of the amino acids that our bodies can make by themselves so we don't really need to worry about eating those. They are called **nonessential amino acids**. There are nine amino acids that we can only get through eating protein-based food. These are called **essential amino acids** because it is essential that we eat them every day to have an adequate amount. It is also important to note that different types of protein sources, such as meat, fish, eggs, dairy, beans, and soy, contain different amounts of each of these amino acids. Choosing our protein sources is very important so that we get the right amount of essential amino acids for our goals, which is to perform the best we possibly can in our sports.

Unit III. Macronutrients Overview (cont.)

Carbohydrate Overview

Carbohydrates, often referred to as just "carbs," are our bodies' preferred source of energy. Carbohydrates supply fuel for all of our daily activities and bodily functions. If proteins were the buildings, think of carbohydrates as the gasoline to transport goods and the electricity that powers all of the buildings. In sports nutrition, the primary function of carbohydrates is to fuel all of our practices and games and still supply enough energy to keep up with all of our normal daily activities. It is important to note that carbohydrates are our bodies' *preferred* source of energy. If none are available, then our bodies also have a back up system to fuel the body known as **ketones**, which are made of fats. Think of ketones as your backup generator; not very efficient, but they can still keep all of the lights on during a storm until the electricity gets turned back on, or in our case, until we find some carbohydrates to eat.

Similar to protein breaking down into smaller pieces called amino acids, carbohydrates can be broken down into simple carbohydrates and complex carbohydrates. **Simple carbohydrates**, or commonly known as **sugar**, can be found in fruits, milk, honey, syrups, white bread, and candy. They get their name because they can be broken down very quickly in the stomach so that our bodies can use them for energy very quickly. Candy is the easiest example to talk about. Candy has a lot of sugar, or simple carbs, compacted into small little pieces. After eating it, you almost immediately can find yourself in a "sugar high" where you fidget more or even feel like bouncing off the walls with energy.

Most of our lives we've been told to avoid sugar or simple carbohydrates, mainly because it is very easy to overeat. If we eat too much, it can cause some health problems. For sports and performance, however, simple carbohydrates, or sugar, can be a useful tool to almost immediately provide a large amount of energy for our practice or sport activity. Too much of anything is bad for you, so this book will avoid talking about what is "good" and what is "bad." It will mostly explain how to use different foods as tools in your tool belt to enhance your sports performance and make sure you perform your best on the court or field. One of the best examples of when simple carbohydrates would be a great tool for an athlete is right before a wrestling match or 200-meter sprint. Bananas, honey, maple syrup, or candy are super fast and easy to digest so that within minutes of eating them, you feel more energized and ready for your sprint or wrestling match. Since simple carbs are so easy and light to digest, they wouldn't sit on your stomach and slow you down the same way a bunch of beans or whole wheat toast would.

Complex carbohydrates, on the other hand, are commonly known as **starches** and **fiber**. The most common complex carbohydrates are present in whole grain wheat, legumes, and vegetables. Complex carbs typically include a lot of fiber, which slows down the digestion process for the carbs so that our bodies can't break them down for energy as quickly. Since they are bigger molecules (where the "complex" comes from) and have fiber attached to them, our bodies have to spend a lot more time breaking them down to use them as energy. Instead of immediately getting energy, you get slow and sustained energy lasting hours, not minutes, with complex carbohydrates. For day-to-day activities, this is great. Some whole wheat toast or beans with breakfast can keep your stomach full for hours and provide enough energy for you to go to school, talk to friends, do homework, and run around if you need to.

Unit III. Macronutrients Overview (cont.)

Complex carbohydrates are thought to be the more healthy carbohydrates because they support digestion, heart health, and lead to less blood sugar highs and lows for diabetics. They also help people lose weight because the fiber keeps people feeling full longer. Simple carbohydrates are broken down very quickly so people are hungry again pretty quickly, making it great for gaining weight but very poor for weight loss. Complex carbohydrates are a useful tool for weight loss, weight maintenance, and moderate intensity exercise. If you've ever heard of "carb loading" the day before a football game or race, this is typically what people are talking about. They'll eat a lot of complex carbs that will take all night to digest and store inside the body as **glycogen** so that the athlete can use it the following day during their sports activity.

After eating carbohydrate-based foods, our bodies break down the carbs into **glucose**. Glucose is then absorbed into the bloodstream and can either be used as energy immediately, like if muscles are actively working during a sporting event, or they get transported to the liver and get stored as glycogen. Like an electrical power grid, the energy is waiting there until the city needs it, and then it will transport the energy back to whatever organ or tissue needs energy. Simple carbohydrates and complex carbohydrates all get stored exactly the same way. The only difference is the speed at which they get stored. Simple sugars get broken down and stored very quickly for fast energy or storage, and complex carbohydrates get broken down very slowly for use or storage. This is why if someone has low blood sugar, they are often given candy or fruit to restore their blood sugar quickly. If someone wants to maintain a stable blood sugar level, they would eat complex carbohydrates so that there is less of an immediate high and more of a slow and steady high in the bloodstream.

Glucose Storage

Our liver and our muscles store all of the glucose in our body. The more muscle you have, the more you can store inside your muscles. In general, we can store about 100–120 grams of glycogen (stored glucose) in our liver. Since there are 4 calories per gram in carbohydrates, that equates to about 400–480 calories (4 x 100–120) of energy stored in our liver. The energy in our liver is typically used for brain energy and organ energy. Our muscle stores vary depending on the person, but an average adult can store 300–400 grams (1,200–1,600 calories) of glycogen in their muscle mass. Athletes can hold even greater glycogen, ranging from 600–700 grams (2,400–2,800 calories) in their muscles.

By adding the two storage sites together, our bodies can store about 1,600–2,000 calories of energy, with athletes sometimes being much higher. This is important because if you eat more carbohydrates than you can store in your liver and muscles, your body goes through a process that converts the sugar into fat, and it is stored as **adipose tissue**, or body fat. Too much body fat slows down our performance if speed or endurance is our goal. If powerlifting or brute force, like shot put or a football lineman, is our goal, then having higher levels of body fat can definitely be an advantage, making it easier to block and push other players around.

Understanding glycogen storage will be a key factor for anyone whose sport depends on a weight class. Each gram of glycogen is stored with and attaches to 3–4 grams of water, which is why high-carb diets can cause temporary weight gain due to glycogen and water retention.

Unit III. Macronutrients Overview (cont.)

500 grams of glycogen is about 1 pound of tissue stored on the body. Since each gram of glycogen attaches to 3–4 grams of water, we can lose 2.5–4.5 additional pounds of water to lower our body weight to make weight for our sporting activity. Just from depleting carbohydrates, an athlete can lose 4–8 pounds of temporary weight, which could be an advantage if they had to weigh in lighter than they typically are. This is safe for most healthy individuals, but very hard to adhere to as it will typically take several days of no carbohydrates to fully deplete glycogen levels. Furthermore, without sugar, your body loses its best source of energy for the sporting event. This will make refueling after the weigh-in with simple carbohydrates vital if the athlete doesn't want to perform worse for the event. This can be another tool in the toolbox that has some benefits but also carries some performance risks. Just note that this method is temporary and very sport-specific.

Fat Overview

Fats, or lipids, are very energy-dense nutrients that provide long-term, low-intensity fuel. They also support cell membrane structure and help absorb key vitamins like A, D, E, and K. They also play a vital role in hormone production, brain insulation, and protecting our organs and our bodies against times of famine or cold, similar to bears during hibernation. In our Lego® city, fats have a very diverse role. Some are like the cars that transport packages throughout the city via hormones in our bloodstream, sending signals to turn different functions on and off. Some build up a protective wall all around the city to separate itself from other cities, such as the cell membrane. The subcutaneous fat right underneath our skin protects us from the cold, and the visceral body fat insulates our organs, similar to wrapping bubble wrap around each of the cities to help protect them from bumps. What's even cooler with fats is that they can provide our bodies with fuel for days or weeks at a time if we can't find food, whereas carbohydrates, our preferred source of energy, could only last hours on its own.

Just like protein and carbohydrates come from the food you eat, so does dietary fat. When you eat things like nuts, butter, avocados, oils, cream, fish, and fatty cuts of meat, they are broken down into **fatty acids** in the stomach and are used to store energy, build cell walls, and protect yourself and your organs. Similar to essential amino acids, some fatty acids are **essential**, which means your body can't make them and they must be consumed from the diet.

Oftentimes, you'll find that most protein foods, such as beef, lamb, fish, and cottage cheese, also contain dietary fats, so for omnivores, fats are relatively easy to get into the diet. When we eat food products from animals, we are eating their muscle and body fat, which then in turn helps us stay alive, using them for the same thing in our own bodies. Many animals we eat are called **ruminants**, which are mammals that have four-chambered stomachs. Since they have four times the amount of stomach capacity, they are able to eat things like grass and take the nutrients and turn it into muscle and body fat in their own bodies. Humans only have one stomach with one chamber, making us very poor grass eaters. Luckily, we're able to shepherd and raise cows, sheep, goats, camel, and deer (some of the healthiest protein sources), which thrive off plants and are able to digest that food for us with their multiple stomach compartments. In turn, we digest them and their byproducts, cream and milk. This is commonly called the "circle of life" and is how herbivores and carnivores, or in our case omnivores, have always interacted

Unit III. Macronutrients Overview (cont.)

in nature. Similar to amino acids and simple/complex carbohydrates, dietary fats can be broken down into unsaturated fats, saturated fats, and trans fat.

Dietary Fats

Fats, also called lipids, are nutrients broken down from dietary fat. **Dietary fat** just means that you get it through your diet, versus body fat or adipose tissue, which is fat that you have already stored inside your own body. There are different kinds of dietary fats, specifically saturated fats and unsaturated fats.

Saturated fats are fats that are usually solid at room temperature. You can find saturated fats in butter, cheese, whole milk, ice cream, beef, pork, and chicken. Saturated fats have many important jobs including providing energy, keeping cell walls solid so that they don't break and cause the cells to die, and supporting hormones, including estrogen and testosterone; these are two of the most important hormones triggering adulthood in teenagers and playing huge roles in sports and performance. It is important to keep the amount of saturated fats balanced within your diet. Since they are solid at room temperature, it's easy to think about them like bricks on the city road. Too many bricks, and the roads, your blood vessels, can start to get clogged, which makes it harder for your heart to pump blood and keep traffic moving. There's a healthy balance between transporting these building blocks to the walls of the city and piling too many blocks up on one road, which could cause some damage, block up traffic, and wouldn't be good for your body.

Unsaturated fats are typically liquid at room temperature and include many types of oils, butters, and fish. Unsaturated fats come from olive oil, avocados, nuts, seeds like chia or sunflower, fish, canola oil, peanut oil, and flaxseed oil, as well as peanut, cashew, and almond butter. Since they're liquid at room temperature, they don't block up roads as easily as saturated fats so your risk of plugging up your veins and arteries goes down due to their flexibility in the bloodstream. Unsaturated fats have very important roles such as powering your brain, helping you think quickly and learn new motor skills, which is very important for all sports activities. In fact, around 60% of your brain is fat, and unsaturated fats keep it running quickly and efficiently. While cell membranes have to be strong enough to keep out intruders, it is also important that they're flexible enough to let goods come in and trash go out of the "city." One specific type of fatty acid is called **omega-3 fatty acid** and is found in fish oil, krill oil, and algae. This keeps our brains smart and efficient and is actually one of the key factors evolutionary scientists believe took our brains from the level of chimpanzees to modern-day super computers capable of reading and writing.

The hormonal aspect of dietary fats is very important. Dietary fats support healthy levels of testosterone and estrogen. **Testosterone** is a hormone responsible for making you grow faster, stronger, and have the energy ready to crush it on the field or court. Biological males have higher levels of testosterone, which is one of the reasons they typically have more muscle mass than females, but females also need healthy levels of testosterone to support muscle growth and function. Testosterone tells your muscles to grow stronger, which will make you faster, more powerful, and stronger so you can shoot a basketball farther, hit a softball farther, jump higher, or throw a ball farther. It also boosts recovery, increases energy and focus, and supports healthy bone growth. **Estrogen**, on the other hand, is usually thought to be a female hormone, but in

Unit III. Macronutrients Overview (cont.)

reality, men need it as well, just in lower quantities. Estrogen makes your bones tougher and stronger, supports muscle recovery, maintains flexibility and joint health, and regulates energy use. Estrogen levels also help support coordination and balance, which are crucial for sports performance.

Every pound of adipose tissue, or stored body fat, contains roughly 3,600 calories. That is enough energy to jog approximately 30 miles for most people, if not more. The average adult can store anywhere from 77,000–157,000 calories of fat on their body. If we typically burn 2,000 calories per day, that means we could survive just off of our stored body fat for 38–78 days if we had adequate levels of hydration available. Our body will always use up our stored glycogen first, roughly 1,600 calories of energy, but then will begin burning our stored adipose tissue as fuel until we can eat our next meal. This is why we don't just simply "shut down" from lack of energy when we haven't eaten a meal for a while. With this being said, if we get too low in body fat, our body will begin to slow down its processes. We will have low energy, and our hormones will decrease, making us feel tired, lethargic, and sick. We will slowly deteriorate and sports performance will decrease. That is why you must always have some body fat tissue on you, even if magazines like to show models with extremely low body fat percentages. Low body fat percentage is not sustainable or advisable for sports and performance or for a healthy life. How you feel is much more important than how you look in the mirror.

Different sports require different levels of body fat. For gymnasts, body fat is kept lower so that they can continue making their jumps higher with less effort. For rugby, having a higher body fat percentage will protect against hard tackles and also help the player tackle other players harder. Too much, and they might be too slow to run with the ball. Too little, and they would get hurt after every tackle. Maintaining a healthy body fat percentage is another useful tool in the tool kit for an athlete and oftentimes changes when in season and out of season. Powerlifters, wrestlers, and fighters will gain a lot of weight in the off-season, trying to maximize recovery and muscle growth (which requires extra calories). They will then lean up and drop weight for the season so that they can make their weight class but still be as athletic and strong as possible. Weight maintenance and management is a tool we will discuss later in this book.

Summary

Food is ingested and then broken down into macronutrients called protein, carbohydrates, and fats. Different foods contain different amounts of these macronutrients. Protein (essential) is broken down into amino acids, which can be used for muscle repair, neurotransmitters, and to keep you healthy on and off the field. Carbohydrates, either simple or complex, can be used as either quick energy or slow and steady energy for daily activities, practices, and sporting events. Dietary carbohydrates (nonessential) can also be manipulated for brief weight loss as a tool to safely adjust weight for weight class activities. Dietary fat helps support your hormones and brain function, protects your body, and gives you nearly limitless amounts of energy in times of famine. Now that you understand the importance of each of the macronutrients, it will be easier to tailor dietary nutrients to your specific needs as an athlete to gain muscle, lose body fat, make weight classes, or stick to a specific weight for your sport, and perform optimally.

Name: ______________________________ Date: ______________________

Unit III. Macronutrients Overview (cont.)

Activity 4: Scavenger Hunt—Get to Know Your Local Shopping Center

For this activity, listed below are the 10 most common protein sources, 5 simple carbohydrate sources, 5 complex carbohydrate sources, 5 saturated fat sources, and 5 unsaturated fat sources. Go to your local shopping center or super market and find each of the products listed. List the name and brand of the product then turn the package over to the nutrition label. Find where the label says calories, carbohydrates, protein, and fat per serving. Fill in the chart below. There are no right answers for this activity; some of you will choose chicken wings and some might choose a chicken breast. Just write the names of whatever you choose and practice finding the calories and macronutrients of each. If the package does not list all the information, look up that type of food online when you get back home to find the nutritional information needed. Try to use things you actually would or consistently eat. Compare with other students so that you can find different foods and recognize how some are higher in calories and lower in calories, some are higher in protein and lower in protein, etc. These will be useful tools down the road!

Protein

Protein Food	Calories	Protein	Carbohydrates	Fat
Beef:				
Chicken:				
Eggs:				
Fish:				
Milk:				
Cheese:				
Whey:				
Yogurt:				
Beans:				
Soy:				

Simple Carbohydrates

Simple Carb Food	Calories	Protein	Carbohydrates	Fat
Fruit:				
Syrups:				
White Bread:				
Candy:				
Milk:				

Name: ______________________ Date: ______________

Unit III. Macronutrients Overview (cont.)

Complex Carbohydrates

Complex Carb Food	Calories	Protein	Carbohydrates	Fat
Whole Wheat:				
Oats:				
Green Vegetables:				
Colorful Vegetables:				
Legumes:				

Saturated Fats

Saturated Fat Food	Calories	Protein	Carbohydrates	Fat
Butter:				
Cheese:				
Milk:				
Pork:				
Lamb:				

Unsaturated Fats

Unsaturated Fat Food	Calories	Protein	Carbohydrates	Fat
Oils:				
Nuts:				
Avocados:				
Fish:				
Nut Butter:				

Unit IV. Micronutrients Overview

Micronutrients Overview

Micronutrients are essential vitamins and minerals required in small amounts for various bodily functions. *Macro* means large, so macronutrients are nutrients required in large amounts (protein, carbohydrates, and fats) in order to maintain bodily functions. *Micro*, meaning small, on the other hand, are nutrients that are needed in small amounts to keep all of the millions of things going on in our bodies running smoothly. Micronutrients can be further broken down into two categories: **vitamins** and **minerals**. Together, micronutrients support processes like immune function, energy production, bone health, and oxygen transport. Not having enough of these vitamins (a **deficiency**) or having too much can cause health issues.

The majority of micronutrients come naturally from whole foods such as meat, fruits, vegetables, dairy, and whole grains. When foods are heavily processed or cooked too long, they typically lose some, if not all, of their micronutrients. Heat, light, refining of grain, and sometimes even air can lower the amount of vitamins C, B, A, and E. Take a frozen meat lover's pizza, for example. The grain used for the dough has been heavily refined and has lost almost all of its B vitamins. The cheese and meat have also been processed, ground, and cooked at a high temperature, lowering the amount of B vitamins and vitamins A and E. Magnesium, potassium, and calcium are also typically removed during grain **refining** (breaking down grain in order to turn it into chewable bread). As a general rule of thumb, the more food goes through different processes to get to your dinner table, the more the key micronutrients have been stripped out of it. This means while we are technically eating enough food and getting enough macronutrients to survive, we typically aren't eating enough micronutrients in order to run all of those underlying processes in our bodies to thrive as athletes. Our goal as athletes is not only to survive, but to grow to our highest potential, gain muscle mass, and perform as well as possible in our preferred sports. In order to do this, we will need to eat as many whole foods, or **nutrient-dense** (high in micronutrients) foods as possible.

Vitamins

Vitamins play many important roles in the body. There are two types of vitamins, water soluble and fat soluble. **Water soluble vitamins** are those that your body can't easily store so whatever your body can't utilize at that time will be urinated out. This is why urine can sometimes look bright neon yellow after taking a multivitamin. Whatever your body doesn't use will be urinated out. This comes in handy because it is extremely hard to overdose on water soluble vitamins, but it also means that you'll have to take these vitamins multiple times per day to make sure that you're getting enough to truly thrive as an athlete. Water soluble vitamins are vitamin C and all of the B vitamins.

Fat soluble vitamins are vitamins that can be stored inside your body fat cells. Like we mentioned before, your body fat stores a lot of energy and also makes up a barrier protecting your body. This barrier is called **subcutaneous fat**, or the body fat right underneath the skin.

Unit IV. Micronutrients Overview (cont.)

One of its jobs is also to store all your fat soluble vitamins, such as vitamins A, D, E, and K. If your body fat percent gets too low, then you will deplete all of your fat soluble vitamins. This is why it's important to maintain healthy levels of body fat and not get too lean. The upside to fat soluble vitamins is they can be stored for long term use so if you don't get enough one day, then you won't feel very different the next day because your body can just utilize what's already stored. The downside, however, is that if you do become deficient, it can take much longer to raise your levels. Many doctors will run a blood test to check for vitamin and mineral deficiencies if you have some ongoing health issues. They will often prescribe vitamins if you are deficient or not getting enough from your diet.

Vitamins: What They Do and Where to Find Them

Vitamin	What it Does	Main Jobs	Sports Performance	Found In	Deficiency Signs
Vitamin A (Retinol)	Helps you see, keeps skin healthy, fights germs	Helps eyes see in the dark, keeps skin smooth, boosts immune system	Keeps eyes sharp for tracking fast moving objects (like a ball), supports quick recovery from cuts and scrapes	Beef liver, salmon, eggs, butter, cheese, dark leafy greens, sweet potatoes, carrots	Night blindness, dry skin, weak immune system, frequently sick
Vitamin D (Calciferol)	Makes bones strong, helps immune system, supports hormones including testosterone and estrogen	Pulls calcium into your bones, helps your body fight sickness, helps fight against autoimmune disorders	Stronger bones reduce injury risk, improves muscle strength and coordination for jumps and sprints	Sunlight, salmon, sardines, egg yolks, beef liver, milk products, mushrooms	Weak bones leading to fractures, muscle weakness, tiredness, bone pain
Vitamin E (Tocopherol)	Protects cells, keeps skin and blood healthy	Stops damage to cells, keeps blood vessels strong	Protects muscles from damage during intense workouts, reduces soreness after exercise	Almonds, sunflower seeds, spinach, avocados, oils, salmon, trout, chicken thighs, egg yolks, grass-fed beef	Muscle weakness, trouble balancing, nerve problems such as tingling
Vitamin K (Phylloquinone, menaquinone)	Helps blood clot, keeps bones strong	Stops bleeding when you get cut, helps build bones	Prevents excessive bleeding from sports injuries, supports bone strength for high-impact sports	Kale, spinach, broccoli, fermented soy, eggs, chicken, cheese, beef liver	Easy bruising, cuts bleed for longer times, weak bones

Unit IV. Micronutrients Overview (cont.)

Vitamins: What They Do and Where to Find Them (cont.)

Vitamin	What it Does	Main Jobs	Sports Performance	Found In	Deficiency Signs
Vitamin C (Ascorbic Acid)	Heals cuts, fights germs, keeps skin strong, keeps tendons and ligaments healthy	Makes skin and gums healthy, helps your body fight colds	Speeds up healing of bruises and injuries, boosts energy for longer workouts by reducing fatigue	Bell peppers, oranges, strawberries, kiwi	Slow wound healing, bleeding gums, tiredness, frequent colds
Vitamin B1 (Thiamine)	Gives you energy, helps your nervous system work	Turns food into energy, keeps nervous system and muscles working together	Boosts energy for endurance sports (like running, swimming, and cycling), improves muscle response for quick movements	Pork, liver, eggs, fish, chicken, brown rice, oatmeal, beans	Tiredness, weak muscles, confusion, poor coordination
Vitamin B2 (Riboflavin)	Gives you energy, keeps skin and eyes healthy	Helps make energy from food, keeps eyes and skin clear	Provides energy for intense sports, protects eyes for better focus during games	Beef liver, eggs, milk, yogurt, spinach, almonds, mushrooms	Cracked lips, sore throat, tired eyes, skin rashes
Vitamin B3 (Niacin)	Gives you energy, keeps skin healthy	Turns food into energy, keeps skin from getting dry	Fuels muscles for longer practices, supports fast recovery after workouts	Chicken, tuna, beef liver, peanuts, mushrooms, brown rice	Skin rashes, tiredness, brain fog, upset stomach
Vitamin B5 (Pantothenic Acid)	Helps make energy, supports hormones	Breaks down food for energy, helps make chemicals and hormones in your body	Provides steady energy for sports, helps the body handle stress from tough games	Beef liver, chicken, eggs, mushrooms, avocados, sweet potatoes	Tiredness, muscle cramps, burning feet, stomach pain
Vitamin B6 (Pyridoxine)	Helps brain and blood work correctly	Makes brain chemicals for mood and helps make red blood cells	Improves focus and mood for better performance, supports oxygen delivery to muscles	Chicken, salmon, beef liver, bananas, chickpeas, potatoes	Mood swings, tiredness, anemia, skin rashes

Unit IV. Micronutrients Overview (cont.)

Vitamins: What They Do and Where to Find Them (cont.)

Vitamin	What it Does	Main Jobs	Sports Performance	Found In	Deficiency Signs
Vitamin B7 (Biotin)	Keeps hair, skin, and nails healthy	Helps use food for energy, makes hair and nails strong	Supports energy for workouts, keeps skin healthy despite sweat and gear friction	Eggs, beef liver, salmon, avocados, walnuts, almonds	Hair loss, brittle nails, skin rashes, tiredness
Vitamin B9 (Folate)	Helps new cells, good for blood	Helps your body grow new cells, makes healthy blood	Supports muscle growth and repair, ensures blood carries oxygen well for stamina	Beef liver, eggs, spinach, kale, lentils, asparagus	Tiredness, anemia, mouth sores, poor growth
Vitamin B12 (Cobalamin)	Keeps nerves and blood healthy	Helps make red blood cells, keeps nerves working	Boosts energy and stamina by supporting blood flow, improves nerve signals for quick reflexes	Clams, beef liver, salmon, eggs, milk	Tiredness, pale skin, numbness/ tingling, memory problems

Listed above are all of the vitamins and their chemical names. When reading nutrition labels, sometimes people get scared when they see the word "acid" and decide that food is not good for them. Well, several of the vitamins (B5 and C for example) contain the name acid in their chemical name and should not be avoided. Context matters when looking at nutrition labels so if you're unsure about something, look it up. Listed in the column "Found In" are all the whole foods that that vitamin can be found in. Some companies add in vitamins, a process known as **fortification**, to make the food higher in vitamins so that consumers buy that food thinking it is a nutrient-dense food. Sugary cereals are known for adding in vitamins to make them seem more nutritious. This is very misleading because while they do add vitamins to the foods, sometimes they are in forms that your body can't use very well. Also, foods high in sugar can deplete vitamins or make it harder for them to do their jobs. For example, high sugar consumption can impair vitamins C, B1, B3, and D from doing their jobs. So if a bowl of fruity cereal says it has a ton of vitamins, the sugar content blocks out many of these vitamins from even being used in the first place. This gives the consumer, you, false confidence that you're getting enough vitamins through those types of foods. It explains how even though you seem to be getting enough, you may still have signs and symptoms of a deficiency. For this reason, it is best to eat whole foods and stay away from too many processed foods for athletic purposes. As a general rule of thumb, 80% of the food you eat should be whole food and 20% can be processed—the **80/20 principle**.

Unit IV. Micronutrients Overview (cont.)

Minerals

Minerals are tiny, tiny nutrients your body needs to stay strong and perform at its best. Vitamins are **organic compounds** coming from living things, whereas **minerals** are **inorganic nutrients** (meaning they come from the earth) that we get from plants or animals that eat or use water, soil, or rocks in their diets. Your body uses minerals for things like building bones, carrying oxygen, and keeping your muscles and nervous system working properly. Similar to vitamins, minerals can be broken down into two groups: **major minerals** (needed in larger amounts, like calcium and magnesium), and **trace minerals** (needed in tiny amounts, like iron and zinc).

Major minerals are stored in the bones, muscles, and other tissues, and your body pulls from these when needed. If your body needs calcium, it will break down its own bones to get it. This is typically not good because your bones can begin to break down, increasing your risk of fractures. It's important to eat a diet high in major minerals so that your body can continue to grow and not have to essentially eat away at itself. We lose a lot of minerals through sweat and hard work, making it vital to replace during our workouts. Calcium, phosphorus, magnesium, sodium, potassium, chloride, and sulfur are the major minerals.

Trace minerals are used in smaller amounts, but they are just as important. They play crucial roles in enzyme activity, bone health, immune function, fighting off infections, thyroid health so you have energy, and carrying oxygen for endurance sports. Trace minerals include iron, zinc, iodine, selenium, copper, manganese, fluoride, chromium, and molybdenum.

For athletes, minerals help you stay energized and recover faster. Similar to vitamins, diets high in processed foods or sugar can block many of the minerals from being absorbed properly. This can cause deficiencies, and it could take some time to rebuild properly, making blood tests to check your mineral levels that much more important when you're feeling ill or not quite yourself.

Minerals: What They Do and Where to Find Them

Mineral	What it Does	Main Jobs	Sports Performance	Deficiency Signs	Found In
Calcium	Builds strong bones and teeth, helps muscles move	Makes bones tough, helps muscles contract, keeps heart beating	Builds stronger bones to prevent fractures, provides better muscle power for sprints and lifts	Weak bones (fractures), muscle cramps, tingling hands, irregular heartbeat	Milk, yogurt, cheese, sardines, kale, broccoli, almonds
Phosphorus	Strengthens bones, gives energy	Builds bones with calcium, helps make energy from food	Supports bone strength for high impact sports, fuels muscles for endurance	Weak bones, muscle weakness, tiredness, loss of appetite	Beef, chicken, salmon, tuna, eggs, dairy, pumpkin seeds, beans, whole grains

Unit IV. Micronutrients Overview (cont.)

Minerals: What They Do and Where to Find Them (cont.)

Mineral	What it Does	Main Jobs	Sports Performance	Deficiency Signs	Found In
Magnesium	Helps muscles relax, supports mental health relaxation, supports energy	Relaxes muscles after work, turns food into energy, calms nerves	Prevents cramps during workouts, boosts energy for longer practices	Muscle cramps, tiredness, irritability, shaky hands	Mackerel, salmon, spinach, almonds, pumpkin seeds, avocados, dark chocolate
Sodium	Balances fluids, helps nerves and muscles	Keeps water in balance, helps muscles contract, sends nerve signals	Maintains hydration for endurance, supports quick muscle responses	Muscle cramps, dizziness, tiredness, nausea (common in those who sweat heavily)	Shrimp, crab, cheese, poultry, pickles, processed foods and meats
Potassium	Controls fluids, helps heart and muscles	Balances water in cells, keeps heart rhythm steady, helps muscles work	Prevents cramps, supports heart for intense cardio, aids recovery	Muscle weakness, cramps, irregular heartbeat, tiredness	Salmon, chicken, beef, bananas, avocados, sweet potatoes
Chloride	Balances fluids, aids digestion	Keeps body fluids stable, helps make stomach acid for digestion	Maintains hydration for long games, supports digestion for energy	Nausea, tiredness, muscle weakness (rare, often tied to sodium loss)	Seafood, eggs, dairy, seaweed, olives, celery
Sulfur	Supports skin, hair, and joints	Builds strong skin and joints, helps detoxify body	Builds stronger joints for high-impact sports, supports healthier skin despite sweat	Brittle hair, weak nails, joint pain (rare, diet usually sufficient)	Eggs, beef, chicken, fish, garlic, onions, broccoli, cabbage
Iron	Carries oxygen, gives energy	Moves oxygen in blood, keeps muscles energized	Boosts stamina for running or cycling, prevents fatigue during games	Tiredness, pale skin, anemia, shortness of breath	Beef liver, red meat, chicken, oysters, spinach, lentils

Unit IV. Micronutrients Overview (cont.)

Minerals: What They Do and Where to Find Them (cont.)

Mineral	What it Does	Main Jobs	Sports Performance	Deficiency Signs	Found In
Zinc	Fights germs, heals wounds, supports growth	Boosts immune system, repairs skin, helps cells grow	Enables faster recovery from injuries, supports stronger immunity for consistent training	Slow healing, frequent colds, hair loss, loss of taste	Oysters, beef, crab, chicken, pumpkin seeds, chickpeas, cashews
Iodine	Supports thyroid, controls metabolism	Helps thyroid make hormones, keeps energy steady	Maintains energy for workouts, supports weight control for performance	Tiredness, weight gain, swollen neck (goiter), slow metabolism	Cod, tuna, shrimp, eggs, dairy, iodized salt, seaweed
Selenium	Protects cells, supports thyroid	Fights cell damage, helps thyroid work, boosts immunity	Reduces muscle damage, supports energy for intense sports	Tiredness, weak muscles, hair loss, weak immunity	Brazil nuts, tuna, beef, eggs, mushrooms, whole grains
Copper	Helps make blood, supports energy	Builds red blood cells, helps use iron, gives energy	Improves oxygen delivery for endurance, supports strong connective tissues	Tiredness, pale skin, weak bones, frequent infections	Beef and chicken liver, oysters, crab, sesame seeds, cashews, dark chocolate
Manganese	Supports bones, helps metabolism	Strengthens bones, helps break down food for energy	Makes stronger bones for jumps, supports better energy for long practices	Weak bones, joint pain, poor growth (rare)	Mussels, beef, hazelnuts, pecans, whole grains, pineapple
Chromium	Helps control blood sugar, supports energy	Helps insulin use sugar for energy, supports muscle growth	Stabilizes energy for workouts, aids muscle building for strength sports	Tiredness, sugar cravings, poor blood sugar control (rare)	Beef, turkey, fish, broccoli, whole grains, apples

Unit IV. Micronutrients Overview (cont.)

Athletes lose 1–3 liters of sweat per hour depending on temperature, humidity, and type of activity. Sweat is made up of water and minerals called **electrolytes** that are crucial for muscle contraction and performance. When you lose this much water and electrolytes, **dehydration** occurs. Dehydration reduces performance, increases risk of muscle cramps, dizziness, headaches, fatigue, and confusion, and can lead to overheating such as heat exhaustion and heat stroke. If you are only drinking water to replace the sweat you've lost, you are not replacing the electrolytes, and you are not fixing your dehydration. In fact, you could be making it worse. It is crucial for athletes to replace the sweat they lose with water filled with electrolytes—minerals such as sodium, chloride, potassium, magnesium, and calcium. Find electrolyte packets or drinks that contain most, if not all, of these minerals. Sodium and chloride are the most lost through sweat, so any supplement should have high amounts of these two minerals with potassium, magnesium, and calcium present in lower amounts. If you're craving salty fast food or chips after a workout, your body is trying to replace the electrolytes it lost during practice. It is best to find a calorie-free electrolyte blend to drink during activity so your body doesn't have to use up its own stores of minerals and can simply use those supplied by the packets. Later chapters will discuss hydration during exercise in greater detail.

Bonus Compounds in Whole Foods

In addition to vitamins and minerals, whole foods also contain fiber, phytonutrients, and amino acids. **Fiber** is a plant-based nutrient your body can't digest, but it helps clear out your digestive system. If you think of your stomach and intestines as one giant pipe just passing food along from your mouth to your anus, fiber is what helps push the food through the pipe for you to excrete through feces. It helps you stay full, keeps digestion steady, and stabilizes your blood sugar for stable energy. Fruit and vegetables are the highest in fiber. Fruit is high in sugar like candy but also contains fiber. The fiber in fruit slows down the digestion process, providing a more stable quick energy as opposed to candy. Whole grains, berries, apples, broccoli, carrots, and beans are some of the foods highest in fiber. Choosing these foods will also help keep you full if your sport requires weight loss or weight maintenance. Foods without fiber are fast-digesting and will typically leave you hungry again shortly after eating, making it more difficult to manage your weight.

Phytonutrients are natural compounds in plants that give them color and flavor. They act as antioxidants, protecting your cells from damage and aging and reducing inflammation from stress in the body. They speed up recovery after workouts as well. Eating the rainbow ensures you get a mix of all the phytonutrients to support your optimal health.

As mentioned previously, **amino acids** are the building blocks of protein that make up all of your muscles and organs. They are essential for muscle growth, repair, and energy. Nine of these are essential because you must get them from food. They help rebuild muscles after training, boost strength, support quick reflexes, and keep your joints strong. These are found in the highest concentrations in meat, dairy, and fish but can also be found in some plants like quinoa, soy, beans, and rice.

Unit IV. Micronutrients Overview (cont.)

Following the 80/20 rule—80% whole foods like meat, veggies, grains, and fruit and 20% processed foods—will fuel your performance and help make sure that you aren't deficient in vitamins, minerals, fiber, phytonutrients, or amino acids.

Vitamin and Mineral Summary

Chances are you will not remember all of the vitamins' and minerals' jobs, functions, and signs and symptoms of deficiency right away. Use this book and refer back to it when issues do come up, and over time, you will get better at troubleshooting your own problems. Vitamin and mineral deficiency have been linked to many major diseases and autoimmune diseases. The downside is that many of the signs and symptoms are similar so it's hard to tell if you are tired because you're deficient in B vitamins or you're low in potassium and sodium, for example. Luckily, many of the foods you would eat to fix a B-vitamin deficiency would also help fix a sodium and potassium deficiency. There is a HUGE overlap between whole food sources so that chances are, you don't have to know exactly which vitamin you're deficient in to fix the problem. You can just take a best guess and the chances are at least some of the foods you add in will have overlapping vitamins and minerals and probably help your signs and symptoms. This also highlights the importance of eating a variety of DIFFERENT kinds of plant and animal sources. Some vitamins found in pork (vitamin B1) aren't found in high amounts in beef. Orange vegetables contain a lot of vitamin A and green leafy vegetables don't. Eat the rainbow when it comes to fruit and vegetables and eat a lot of different types of meat (or proteins) to make sure you're not deficient in any one thing.

Get 5–30 minutes of direct sunlight every morning for vitamin D synthesis depending on the time of year and where you live. You don't want to get so much sunlight that you burn, but it is crucial that you get some sunlight for mitochondrial health and vitamin D. If you're worried about wrinkles, use SPF 15 on your face but let as much of your body get the sunlight as possible. The goal is to get just enough so that you aren't deficient in vitamin D, but also not get sunburnt, increasing the risk of skin cancer later. You will develop natural skin protection, through melanation, which will give you some protection from sun damage.

Blood tests for checking your current levels of minerals and vitamins are becoming more and more common and can even be purchased online and sent in to labs. These blood tests can double check if you're deficient in any one area. Prices on blood tests will likely continue to go down as more people start to use them. I recommend getting tests done twice a year for athletes just to make sure they don't have any deficiencies that could lower their performance. Sometimes, eating foods high in a certain vitamin or mineral isn't enough to fix the deficiency. In these cases, supplements will come in handy. You can buy any of these vitamins and minerals in various forms and supplement what your body needs. Due to overdose risk for some vitamins and minerals, the best practice would be to get a blood test, find the deficiency, supplement, and retest to see if the supplement is working and make sure you aren't overdosing. This is best done with medical supervision. Some vitamins and minerals are water soluble, like B vitamins, so they can be added in supplement form with little risk of overdosing. Consult your doctor for blood tests or supplement guidance if you think something might be wrong.

Name: ______________________________ Date: ____________________

Unit IV. Micronutrients Overview (cont.)

Activity 5: Vitamin Match-Up

In the right hand column, you will find the main function and sports performance benefit of the vitamins discussed in the chapter. Use the table from pages 17–19 to find the corresponding vitamin that matches with the main functions in the right column. All vitamins will be used in this activity. Once completed, you can use the chart as a handy reference guide.

Vitamin	Main Functions
1.	Pulls calcium into your bones, helps your body fight sickness, helps fight against autoimmune disorders. Builds stronger bones to reduce injury risk, improves muscle strength and coordination for jumps and sprints.
2.	Stops bleeding when you get cut, helps build bones. Prevents excessive bleeding from sports injuries, supports bone strength for high-impact sports.
3.	Turns food into energy, keeps the nervous system and muscles working together. Boosts energy for endurance sports (like running, swimming, and cycling), improves muscle response for quick movements.
4.	Turns food into energy, keeps skin from getting dry. Fuels muscles for longer practices, supports fast recovery after workouts.
5.	Makes brain chemicals for mood and helps make red blood cells. Improves focus and mood for better performance, supports oxygen delivery to muscles.
6.	Helps your body grow new cells, makes healthy blood. Supports muscle growth and repair, ensures blood carries oxygen well for stamina.
7.	Helps make red blood cells, keeps nerves working. Boosts energy and stamina by supporting blood flow, improves nerve signals for quick reflexes.
8.	Helps use food for energy, makes hair and nails strong. Supports energy for workouts, keeps skin healthy despite sweat and gear friction.
9.	Breaks down food for energy, helps make chemicals and hormones in your body. Provides steady energy for sports, helps the body handle stress from tough games.
10.	Helps make energy from food, keeps eyes and skin clear. Provides energy for intense sports, protects eyes for better focus during games.
11.	Makes skin and gums healthy, helps your body fight colds. Speeds up healing of bruises and injuries, boosts energy for longer workouts by reducing fatigue.
12.	Stops damage to cells, keeps blood vessels strong. Protects muscles from damage during intense workouts, reduces soreness after exercise.
13.	Helps eyes see in the dark, keeps skin smooth, boosts immune system. Keeps eyes sharp for tracking fast moving objects (like a ball), supports quick recovery from cuts and scrapes.

Name: ______________________________ Date: ______________________

Unit IV. Micronutrients Overview (cont.)

Activity 6: Mineral Match-Up

In the right hand column, you will find the main function and sports performance benefit of the minerals discussed in the chapter. Use the table from pages 20–22 to find the corresponding mineral that matches with the main functions in the right column. All minerals will be used in this activity. Once completed, you can use the chart as a handy reference guide.

Mineral	Main Functions
1.	Keeps body fluids stable, helps make stomach acid for digestion. Maintains hydration for long games, supports digestion for energy.
2.	Strengthens bones, helps break down food for energy. Makes stronger bones for jumps, supports better energy for long practices.
3.	Builds bones with calcium, helps make energy from food. Supports bone strength for high impact sports, fuels muscles for endurance.
4.	Builds red blood cells, helps use iron, gives energy. Improves oxygen delivery for endurance, supports strong connective tissues.
5.	Boosts the immune system, repairs skin, helps cells grow. Enables faster recovery from injuries, supports stronger immunity for consistent training.
6.	Fights cell damage, helps thyroid work, boosts immunity. Reduces muscle damage, supports energy for intense sports.
7.	Makes bones tough, helps muscles contract, keeps heart beating. Builds stronger bones to prevent fractures, produces better muscle power for sprints and lifts.
8.	Builds strong skin and joints, helps detoxify the body. Builds stronger joints for high-impact sports, supports healthier skin despite sweat.
9.	Relaxes muscles after work, turns food into energy, calms nerves. Prevents cramps during workouts, boosts energy for longer practices.
10.	Keeps water in balance, helps muscles contract, sends nerve signals. Maintains hydration for endurance, supports quick muscle responses.
11.	Balances water in cells, keeps heart rhythm steady, helps muscles work. Prevents cramps, supports the heart for intense cardio, aids recovery.
12.	Helps insulin use sugar for energy, supports muscle growth. Stabilizes energy for workouts, aids muscle building for strength sports.
13.	Moves oxygen in blood, keeps muscles energized. Boosts stamina for running or cycling, prevents fatigue during games.
14.	Helps thyroid make hormones, keeps energy steady. Maintains energy for workouts, supports weight control for performance.

Unit V. Food as Fuel: Energy Systems for Sports

Energy System Overview

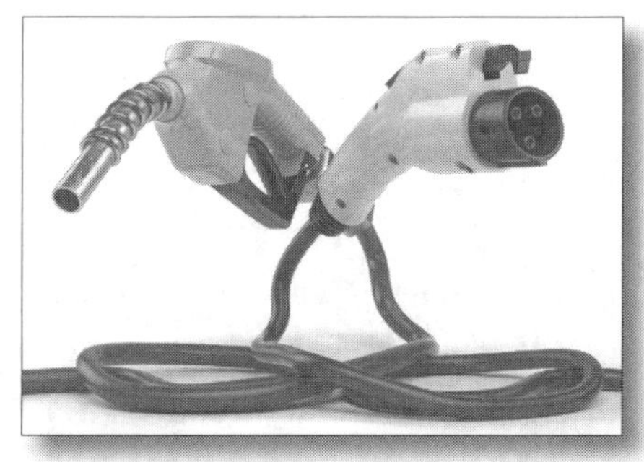

Hybrid cars typically have two energy systems to fuel your drive from point A to point B. They will use the electric battery for in-town transportation with speeds going from 0–40 miles per hour. However, the battery power isn't strong enough to go at a faster pace, 40+ miles per hour, so the car has to switch over to gasoline power to handle higher speeds on the highway. Easy drives utilize the battery, which is relatively cheap to recharge, and fast drives utilize gas, which is more expensive and has more negative byproducts.

The human body is an even more incredible and complex machine. Similar to the hybrid car, we have multiple energy systems for all of our daily activities, depending on how intense they are. In fact, we have **three energy systems** that are constantly fueling our bodies, more like a tribrid engine. **Metabolism** is defined as a chemical process that occurs within an organism in order to maintain life or perform an activity. With cars, we talk about fuel as either being from the battery or gasoline, both are broken down into fuel. In our bodies, our fuel is simply called **ATP (adenosine triphosphate)**, so the more ATP something produces, the more fuel we get out of it. All of our daily activities and sustaining life come down to ATP, or our fuel.

The first energy system is called the **ATP-PC System** and can be thought of as your power system. Activities that require a lot of strength or power in very short bursts rely heavily on this energy system. Unlike normal cars, this energy is like the athletic magic system within the body. This energy system is kind of like if you have a magic button in your car that you can press to turn on the rocket booster NOS system. It will allow you to go super fast super quickly, but you only have about 10 seconds of that 100+ miles per hour speed before the rocket fuel runs out. This energy system is the first energy system you'll use with all of your movements in sports. **The first 0–15 seconds of all activity runs off this energy system**, which is fueled by **phosphocreatine**, or in layman's terms, **creatine**. Think of swinging a baseball bat once, a tennis serve, a shot put, a pole vault, or any other activity that requires a few seconds of a very short burst of maximal power energy.

The second energy system is similar to a gasoline-powered vehicle. It can handle those middle to high speeds of 40 miles per hour to 100 miles per hour but creates more of a byproduct called **lactate**, which can slow down performance and make your muscles feel heavy when too much lactate is produced. This is why you may find yourself running the first two minutes of a mile at a very fast pace but then quickly have to slow down as your muscles start to feel heavy and you start to run out of breath. This energy system is called the **glycolytic energy system**. When your body runs out of creatine after performing its first 0–15 seconds of work, it will switch gears and begin relying on the glycolytic energy system. The glycolytic energy system breaks down **glucose** (the sugar from carbohydrates) to make ATP. This process is called **glycolysis** and is **anaerobic** (which means it does not require oxygen). It powers all of our activities from about 15 seconds to 2 minutes. Think of a 400-meter run, sprinting up and down the soccer field, a fast break on the basketball court, or a 2-minute round of MMA, wrestling, or boxing.

Unit V. Food as Fuel: Energy Systems for Sports (cont.)

After 2 minutes is up, your body produces too much lactate for it to continue at that speed, so your body switches gears again into the **oxidative energy system**, or the **aerobic energy system**. The oxidative system is like long-lasting battery power that can handle low-level activities going from 0–40 miles per hour. Your body uses oxygen to break down primarily **fat**, glucose, and sometimes protein to make a lot of ATP. It is super efficient and produces a ton of energy. You can rely on this energy system for anywhere from 2 minutes to hours worth of activity. The trade off, however, is that you can't go that fast, but you can go for a long time. Think of long-distance walking, running, cycling, or cross country skiing.

As an athlete, you must identify the primary energy systems you will use in your sports so that you can train and eat accordingly to make sure that your body is full of the nutrients it needs to perform at its best. If your diet doesn't include any carbohydrates, then you will not be able to keep up speed on the fast breaks on the football field or basketball court. If your creatine stores aren't full, you won't be able to hit a baseball very far. Knowing these systems will help athletes train smarter. It is important to identify the main energy system your sport relies on so that you can eat or supplement accordingly to optimize your performance.

Putting It All Together: Fuel Your Sport

At this point, you've learned a lot about the energy systems and how to determine what movements or sporting activities belong to each energy system. Intense and short bursts of energy

such as shot put, 40-yard dash, a volleyball serve, or softball swing, all use the creatine phosphate energy system, recycle creatine as fuel, and make up the first 0–15 seconds of all movement. After 15 seconds of consistent movement, your body switches gears to the glycolytic energy system burning carbohydrates (either ingested as glucose or using your body's own stored glycogen and breaking them down into glucose) to take care of sports such as the 200-meter dash, fast breaks on the lacrosse field or basketball court, or a whole play in football. From 15 seconds to 2 minutes, your body will use this energy system for moderate intensity activities. Once your movement surpasses 2 minutes, it can't keep up with the lactate produced in the muscles and will have to switch gears again to oxidizing fat as fuel in the oxidative energy system like with long distance running or cycling. In reality, very few movements in sports use just one energy system. Most likely, they use a combination of all three at different times, but will mostly utilize two of the systems. For breaking down your own sport, in the next activity, you will reference your sport, the primary tasks of the sport, the primary energy system used, and the accessory energy system used. Identifying the different energy systems and the different fuel requirements for each energy system used in your sport will shape how you eat during the season and leading up to the individual games.

Summary: Fuel Your Engine With the Right Food

Phosphate Creatine Energy System (ATP-PC): Your body relies on creatine for energy within this energy system. Creatine is naturally found in red meat and fish. However, to saturate your muscles fully with creatine (AKA keep the fuel tank on FULL for your sport), you would probably

Unit V. Food as Fuel: Energy Systems for Sports (cont.)

have to eat between 2–3 pounds of red meat per day. For this reason, creatine monohydrate supplementation has been the most widely studied supplement in exercise science. It has been found to be effective in filling up this energy tank and is safe for teens, adults, and older adults with healthy kidney function. Creatine has undergone thorough testing and is even showing huge health benefits with diabetes, dementia, Alzheimer's, fall prevention, and many other diseases. Always consult with your physician before starting any supplement regime.

Glycolytic (anaerobic) Energy System: The glycolytic energy system burns the fuel that sounds exactly like the name: glucose and glycogen (your body's stored glucose). Your body breaks down dietary carbohydrates into their most basic form, glucose, and either uses it for glycolytic energy or stores it as glycogen. Remember back to how much glycogen we store in our liver and muscles. The glycolytic energy system will burn up these stored carbohydrates (glycogen). Carbs are king, so if your sport relies heavily on the glycolytic energy system for the moderate level 15 seconds to 2 minutes worth of activity before taking a break (similar to a basketball fast break or soccer fast break), your diet should consist of a lot of pasta, rice, quinoa, oatmeal, fruit, potatoes, whole wheat bread, and other carbohydrate-based foods. This is why football and soccer teams will typically carb load the night before a big game to make sure that the athletes are fully saturated with carbohydrates stored as glycogen in their bodies so that they can perform their best.

Oxidative (cardiovascular-based) Energy System: The oxidative (requiring oxygen) energy system burns fuel slow and steady at a low intensity but is almost limitless in how long it can provide energy. Oftentimes, your joints or your boredom give out well before this energy system will. For this energy system, your body should predominantly burn fat as fuel, sometimes switching to carbohydrates when intensity requirements go up, like running uphill or trying to keep up with someone else. Luckily, almost every person has thousands of calories of stored body fat on them in their subcutaneous body fat. If you have 10 pounds of body fat, you have approximately 34,000 calories of stored energy for this energy system to use, which is approximately 300 miles worth of running. With that being said, it is also wise to keep your glycogen stores full for when your body has to burn carbohydrates for the more difficult parts of long distance running or cycling (uphills). You also shouldn't let your body fat get too low. If your body fat gets too low, then it won't have as much stored fuel for your runs. Your body needs at least some body fat at all times to keep you alive and keep your hormones optimal. This is called **essential body fat**. Because you should never get thin enough to burn up your essential body fat, you want a cushion of body fat on top of the essential body fat so that you can use it during your races and practices. Too much body fat, however, will slow down your time because you're carrying extra weight on your body. This is a balancing act, but keep a healthy level of body fat for your sport (more will be discussed later on this), and also eat a high carb diet.

Name: ____________________ Date: ____________________

Unit V. Food as Fuel: Energy Systems for Sports (cont.)

Activity 7: Energy System Analysis by Sport

For this activity, you will write down three of your own athletic sports or hobbies. You will then think about the tasks required to perform each sporting activity. Examine the duration of each movement, how many times a movement is performed, and how long of breaks you get in between movements. If you get a quick burst of activity followed by a long break, say a long jump, you will write the primary energy system is phosphate creatine. If your sport is more like the 200–400-meter hurdles, a longer run but with frequent short bursts of energy to hurdle, you will write the primary energy system is the anaerobic energy system and the accessory energy system is the phosphate creatine system. If you are a cross country runner, you will use the oxidative energy system as your primary system with short bursts of anaerobic or phosphate creatine to make it up hills or to sprint at the end to try to beat your opponent. There is no single answer for this activity. There is oftentimes a blend of all three energy systems, and different positions might require different energy systems even within the same sport. The point of the activity is to examine your own tasks, understand what energy system those tasks require, and later you will learn how to eat appropriately to fuel those energy systems.

If you do not play three sports, practice by choosing three athletic activities you like. If you don't have any athletic activities that you like, choose three from the five major high school sports—football, track and field, basketball, volleyball, and soccer—and analyze their movements. Analyze at least three movements following the baseball example. If you need more room, you can use this chart as an example to create a chart on your own paper.

Sport	Tasks	Primary Energy System	Accessory Energy System
Baseball	Hitting, throwing, sprinting short distances; a lot of movement in a short amount of time followed by a couple minutes break	Phosphate Creatine	Anaerobic Energy System (base running)

Unit VI. Body Composition

Body Composition Management Overview

At this point in your life, you have probably heard your parents or other adults talking about wanting to lose weight or gain weight. As athletes, you will have to stay above the fray on weight loss and gain fads and instead, focus on your body composition. **Body composition** is the breakdown of your own body into different parts, such as fat and your skeletal muscle mass (muscle, tendons, ligaments, and bone). Body composition is an important indicator of health, fitness, and nutritional status. Any focus of weight loss should be on losing body fat while minimizing any muscle loss, and usually any focus on gaining weight should be to maximize muscle gain while minimizing fat gain. You can perform best in different sports and even different sporting positions at certain percent body fats.

Percent body fat is the proportion of a person's total body weight that is made up of fat mass and is expressed as a percentage. To calculate percent body fat, you would take your fat mass and divide it by your total body weight and then multiply it by 100.

Formula

Body Fat Percentage = (Fat Mass/Total Body Weight) x 100

Example

You are a 150-pound athlete with 15 pounds of body fat mass
Body Fat Percentage = (15/150) x 100 = 10%
This means that out of all 150 pounds of this athlete, 10% of him/her is body fat.

There are many tools used to calculate your percent body fat. Advances in most weight scales have improved so that they can measure percent body fat using **Bioelectrical Impedance Analysis (BIA)**, which uses a small electrical current throughout the body to measure how much body fat you have. Other tools include skinfold calipers, medical devices such as a DEXA scale, or athletic devices such as hydrostatic weighing and air displacement (bod pods). Calipers and BIA are the cheapest and most readily available tools to use, as other equipment can cost thousands of dollars. I would recommend simply using a BIA device because these can typically be found in modern weight scales, handheld devices, or at many nutrition shops around the country. If you don't have access to one, you can purchase skinfold calipers, which are inexpensive but do require some skill.

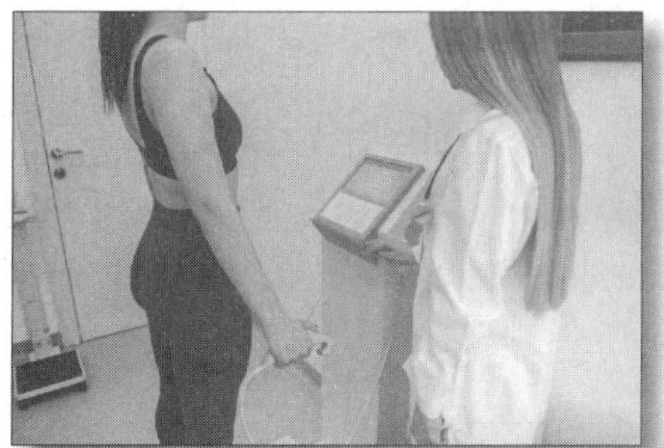

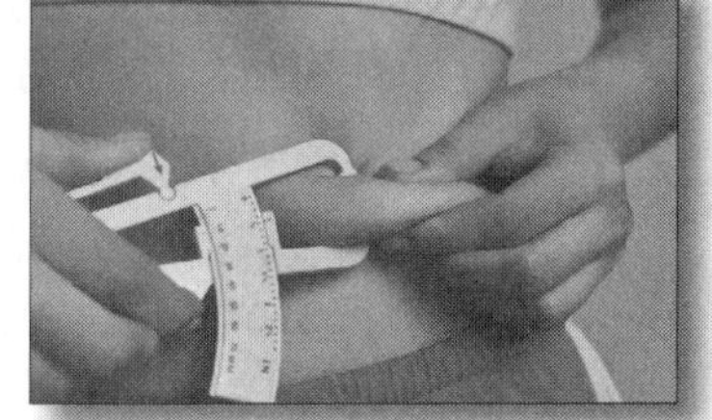

Why Body Composition Matters

Body composition matters quite a bit for sports to optimize athletic performance. Think of your body fat like a weighted vest. As mentioned earlier, if you're 150 pounds and 10% body fat, you are carrying around a 15-pound weight vest. If you are 150 pounds and 30% body fat, you're carrying around a 45-pound weight vest. Who do you think would run a 40-yard dash quicker?

Unit VI. Body Composition (cont.)

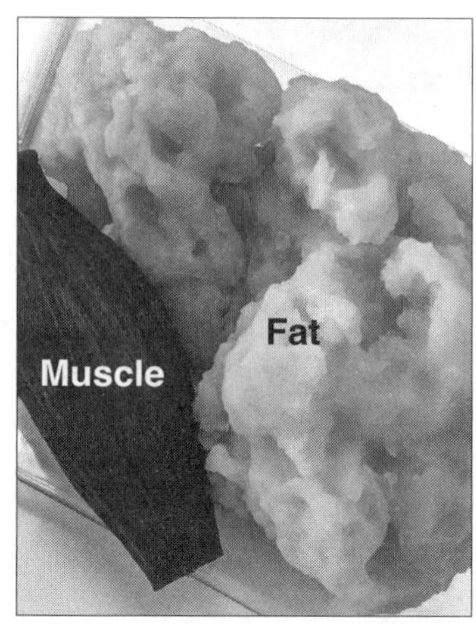

Furthermore, a 150-pound 10% body fat athlete has much more muscle mass than someone of equal weight who has 45 pounds of body fat. In fact, the 10% athlete has 30 pounds more lean body mass (muscle, tendons, ligaments, bone) than the 30% body fat athlete. Body fat and skeletal muscle mass have an inverse relationship, so even if you're the same weight, the lower your body fat, the higher the skeletal muscle mass, and the higher the body fat, the lower the skeletal muscle mass. **Muscle mass** is what creates force and moves your body from point A to point B. It is useful tissue that determines your strength, speed, endurance, agility, and even decreases your risk of injury. Generally, the more muscle you have, the stronger, more powerful, and more athletic you will be.

Some body fat is **essential**, meaning you can never be 0% body fat or you would die. Some body fat is useful too. For instance, football linemen benefit from having extra body fat so they're harder to push around. Some sports like wrestling and powerlifting include weight classes as well. Different people naturally have an easier time at staying at different body weights and might even perform better with higher body fat percentages, making it an advantage for them. Taking a closer look at track athletes, sprinters generally want a lot of leg muscle, which helps them perform better. They will want to minimize body fat because every pound of extra weight will just slow them down. Throwers, however, use the rotational force of their body to throw things very long distances, so a higher body fat percentage for them is useful for building more rotational power and throwing farther. Rather than getting stuck trying to lose or gain "weight," we will focus on how to manage your body composition according to your sport and gender, and focus on building lean muscle so that you can consistently improve your athletic performance.

1. **Performance Optimization:** Low fat enhances speed, lean mass supports strength, and combined, they enhance power and agility.
2. **Sport/Position-Specific Needs:** Different sports and different roles require different compositions to maximize performance.
3. **Injury Prevention:** Balanced composition reduces joint and muscle strains.
4. **Energy Efficiency:** Leaner athletes expend less energy doing normal tasks, which aids in endurance.
5. **Developmental Health:** Having healthy levels of body fat supports puberty and hormones. Being too lean can crash testosterone and estrogen levels and stunt an athlete's growth and development.

Typical Body Fat Ranges for Adults

- **Essential Body Fat:** Males: 2–5%; Females: 10–13%
- **Athletes:** Males: 5–15%; Females 12–20% (varies by sport and position)
- **General Health:** Males 10–20%; Females 20–30%

In order to just stay alive, humans need a baseline level of body fat. Men need less than women. Women need more body fat due to their hormones and reproductive responsibilities involved with carrying and housing a baby during pregnancy. As a general rule of thumb, a male's 10% body fat will be comparable to a female's 18–20%, so a female should never try to chase a male's low level of body fat or she might cause harm to her monthly cycles and hormonal

Unit VI. Body Composition (cont.)

health. On the other hand, with too much body fat, our organs have to work harder to keep us alive, muscles and tendons have to work harder to move us around, and more inflammation builds up in our bodies, which can cause various diseases and autoimmune disorders. Keeping a healthy body composition is far more important than focusing on weight loss or weight gain, which typically doesn't center around muscle mass and body fat. Usually someone trying to lose 100 pounds doesn't care if it's muscle, bone, tendon, ligament, or body fat—they just want the weight off. This is not good thinking because muscle is the longevity organ and will help people live longer, healthier lives. Any weight loss should be focused on a reduction of body fat while saving as much muscle as possible. For this reason, we will focus on percent body fat loss and gain as our primary goal for managing weight in this book, depending on our sports needs and requirements.

Typical Body Fat Ranges by Sport

Sport	Body Fat Percent Range	Why	Example
Football	Linemen: 12–15% Males Skill Positions: 8–12% Males	Linemen require more body fat to help block and tackle, whereas wide receivers need speed, agility, and endurance without extra body fat slowing them down.	A running back with 10% body fat and high muscle mass can accelerate quickly, evade defenders, and maintain endurance on a 40-yard run.
Basketball	Males: 7–12% Females: 12–18%	Enhances agility, vertical jumping for rebounds, endurance for the long duration without timeouts, and speed for fast breaks	A point guard with 8% body fat can swiftly move side to side and up and down the court, while a center with higher body fat can force lighter opponents out of the paint for rebounds.
Track & Field	Sprinters: 6–10% Males, 12–16% Females Distance Runners: 5–9% Males, 10–15% Females Throwers: 12–18% Males, 18–24% Females	Sprinters and runners need less of a weight vest to move quickly and use less energy when they weigh less, improving endurance, while throwers need more mass for rotational power.	A female with 10% body fat weighs less and uses less energy during long runs, which improves endurance and allows her to run longer with less muscle work.
Baseball/ Softball	Males: 8–14% Females: 14–20%	Supports agility, pitching velocity, and bat speed	Outfielders need lower percentages to chase after balls, whereas a catcher needs more muscle and size to block the plate when runners come to home plate.

Unit VI. Body Composition (cont.)

Typical Body Fat Ranges by Sport (cont.)

Sport	Body Fat Percent Range	Why	Example
Soccer	Males: 7–12% Females: 13–18%	Soccer requires speed, agility, and endurance for long matches to handle duration and directional changes.	A midfielder with low body fat has improved endurance and agility, whereas a goalkeeper with a higher percentage doesn't have the same endurance requirements, and the extra mass can help block more shots by taking up space in the goal.
Wrestling	Males: 5–11% Females: 12–18% ***Wrestling uses weight classes. The goal is to minimize fat mass and to maximize lean body mass so that your muscle mass determines what weight class you will be in. Do not sacrifice muscle mass to get into a lower weight class. This will only hinder your growth and development and create eating disorders.**	Wrestlers come in all shapes and sizes. The goal of the off-season should be to put on as much muscle as possible while minimizing their body fat gain, as excess fat reduces agility, and low muscle mass reduces grappling power. Too many athletes starve themselves to make weight during the season and lose most of their muscle. This is a disaster, and more will be discussed next chapter to avoid this pitfall.	A 120-pound wrestler at 6% body fat maximizes muscle leverage and endurance for matches. A 150-pound wrestler at 6% body fat dominates his weight class, even though he's the same percent body fat as the first wrestler. He/she lets their muscle mass determine their weight class.
Volleyball	Males: 7–12% Females: 12–18%	Volleyball requires vertical jumping, agility, and power. Liberos prioritize leanness and agility for diving while middle blockers need more muscle mass to dominate the net.	A female setter with 13% body fat moves quickly to set up plays, while a middle blocker with 15% body fat can still jump high and has more mass to block spikes.
Cross Country	Males: 5–10% Females: 10–15%	Reduces energy expenditure while keeping fatigue down by carrying a very small "weight vest"	A 100-pound runner with 6% body fat carrying around 6 pounds of body fat has an easier and faster pace over a 5k than a runner carrying around an extra 10 pounds of body fat at 10% body fat.

Unit VI. Body Composition (cont.)

Typical Body Fat Ranges by Sport (cont.)

Sport	Body Fat Percent Range	Why	Example
Swimming	Males: 6–12% Females: 12–18%	Lean mass supports propulsion, but some body fat helps with buoyancy and in distance events, especially with women.	A female freestyle sprinter with 13% cuts through water easier and moves faster while a distance swimmer with 15% has more body fat to use as energy and improved buoyancy (fat helps stay afloat) for distance swims.
Gymnastics	Males: 5–10% Females: 10–16%	Gymnasts are known for very low body fat to maximize power-to-weight ratio for flips, vaults, and holds. Carrying too low of a body fat for too long can risk hormonal imbalances, weakened immunity, and frailty. It is recommended that gymnasts do not stay in lower body fat percentage all year long and hang out in the higher percentages while they are not actively competing, saving the lower percent body fat for when they're doing important competitions.	Lower body fat improves power to weight ratio and reduces injuries by not putting so much stress on joints when landing or holding themselves up. Endurance improves, and less energy is wasted during routines.

Body Composition Summary

Your body composition should align with your sport and the needs of your position. As a general rule, increased skeletal muscle mass is a good thing for athletic performance. You will be stronger, more powerful, more agile, in better metabolic health, and more resilient with more muscle mass. What must be managed, however, is your percent body fat. A balanced composition for your sport will prevent joint strain, aid in endurance, and maintain hormonal health so that you do not stunt your normal growth and development and maintenance of your mental health. Focus on what you're made of, body fat or muscle mass (body composition), rather than the "weight."

It is important to note that these body fat percentages by sport are only required during the sport season. Oftentimes athletes find themselves in the high end of their body fat percentage during the off-season. This is normal and will help maximize lean muscle gain while the athlete is training for muscle mass improvements during the off-season.

Name: ______________________________ Date: ______________________

Unit VI. Body Composition (cont.)

Activity 8: Matching Body Fat Percentages

Below, draw lines from each body fat percent range to its appropriate definition.

1. Men's Essential Body Fat	A. 10–13%
2. Women's Essential Body Fat	B. 5–15%
3. Male Athlete Body Fat	C. 2–5%
4. Female Athlete Body Fat	D. 10–20%
5. Male General Health Body Fat	E. 20–30%
6. Female General Health Body Fat	F. 12–20%

Activity 9: Figuring Body Fat Percentages

Use the formula and the numbers given to figure the body fat percentages for each scenario. Round to the nearest tenth if needed.

Formula: (Fat Mass/Total Body Weight) x 100 = Body Fat Percentage

1. A 160-pound person with 20 pounds of body fat mass

   (__________ / __________) x 100 = __________%

2. A 125-pound person with 12 pounds of body fat mass

   (__________ / __________) x 100 = __________%

3. A 97-pound person with 12 pounds of body fat mass

   (__________ / __________) x 100 = __________%

4. A 143-pound person with 22 pounds of body fat mass

   (__________ / __________) x 100 = __________%

5. A 176-pound person with 30 pounds of body fat mass

   (__________ / __________) x 100 = __________%

Unit VII. Improving Your Composition: Muscle Gain & Fat Loss

Muscle Gain & Fat Loss Overview

In an effort to stay above the complexities of all the various weight loss supplements, special diets, and weight loss surgeries, all weight loss can be summed up by creating a **calorie deficit** (that means consistently eating fewer calories than you burn all day), and all weight gain can be summed up by creating a **calorie surplus** (consistently eating more calories than you burn per day). Consistently doing either of these will result in weight loss or weight gain.

Weight loss pills, usually known as **thermogenics**, are typically loaded with supplements or chemicals that give you short-term energy or blunt (decrease) your hunger. More short-term energy means you burn more calories, and less hunger makes it easier to eat less. Ultimately, they help you burn more and eat less, which puts you in a calorie deficit.

Weight loss **peptides** (like the popular Wegovy® or Ozempic® medicines) work by blocking hunger hormones and slowing down your digestion, making it easier to eat less and ultimately putting you into a calorie deficit.

Weight loss surgery, known as **bariatric surgery**, either removes part of your stomach so that you get full faster, or it ties a band around your stomach, making your stomach artificially smaller, and therefore, helping you get full faster. Both of these help create a calorie deficit.

The **ketogenic** or **carnivore diet** completely removes one macronutrient, **carbohydrates**, and fills you up with high-satiety protein and fat so that it makes it more difficult to overeat, which creates a calorie deficit. **Vegan** or **vegetarian diets** completely remove animal foods and focus on filling your stomach with low-calorie, dense, fibrous plant food. This makes it harder to eat high-calorie foods because you're always full on fiber, which helps you stay in a calorie deficit.

People taking **performance enhancing drugs (PEDS)** such as SARMs (Selective Androgen Receptor Modulators), steroids, or peptides for growth, typically report more hunger and a faster digestive system, making it easier to eat more, which puts them in a calorie surplus.

As you can see, all of these fads and interventions ultimately create the same thing: *a calorie deficit or a calorie surplus.* The worst part about all of these interventions is that they typically completely ignore the quality of weight that an individual loses or gains. They don't care if the weight is muscle, fat, bone, tendon, or ligament. There are many downsides to all of these interventions, but by far the most tragic is ignoring body composition. The goal should be to lose body fat, not simply lose weight, or to gain muscle mass, not simply gain weight. By losing body fat, you still maintain the function and health benefits of a higher muscle mass. As athletes, this will be your challenge—to slowly, incrementally increase muscle mass year after year so you can improve your athletic performance, while minimizing fat gain so that your endurance, speed, agility, power, joint health, and overall athleticism improves.

This chapter combines the lessons learned in Unit II to roughly calculate your calorie needs to maintain weight, gain weight, or lose weight, and takes lessons from Unit III and teaches

Unit VII. Improving Your Composition: Muscle Gain & Fat Loss (cont.)

you about the appropriate macronutrient ratios per day to make sure that the quality of weight you gain is mostly muscle and the quality of weight you lose is mostly body fat. You will use the previous unit as your guide to know what body fat percentage you should have to optimize your athletic performance. This will provide lifelong tools to manage your body composition while minimizing the stress and anxiety that comes with typical weight loss and gain methods.

Calories: Your Budgeting Tool for Weight Management

Thinking back to calories as your income, if you save more than you spend that day, then you will gain money in your checking account. If you spend more money that week than you made, you will have to use money from your savings account, or your own stored body fat and glycogen stores.

Let's pretend that every $0.01 you spend in a day is equivalent to 1 calorie. If you burn 2,000 calories per day through your **TDEE (Total Daily Energy Expenditure)**, that is equivalent to spending $200. If you only made $150 that day at work (only ate 1,500 calories), you did not eat/earn as much as you spent so $150 – $200 = $-50. In calorie terms, that's 1,500 (eaten) – 2,000 (burned) = -500 calories for the day. Well, since you didn't have enough money to cover what you spent, you'll have to go withdraw $50 from your savings account. In your own body, your savings account is your **glycogen** (stored sugar) and **body fat mass** (stored as subcutaneous body fat under your skin or visceral body fat around your organs). If you do this every day for 7 days, you will have had to use $350 from your savings account or 3,500 calories, which is equivalent to 1 pound of weight. If you do this for 4 weeks, you will have lost 4 pounds of weight. If you do this for three months, you will have lost 12 pounds of weight. That is how your body loses weight, by consistently taking in fewer calories than you spend on activity, or burning more calories than you take in. This is a **calorie deficit**.

On the other hand, if you only spent $200 but you made $250, or burned 2,000 calories but ate 2,500 calories, you will have added $50 or 500 calories to your savings account. If you do this every day for a week, you will have gained 1 pound of weight. If you do this every day for a month, you will have gained 4 pounds. If you do it for three months, you will have gained 12 pounds. This is a **calorie surplus**.

Adjustments may need to be made to make sure you're gaining or losing at a steady weight. As you learned in Unit II, the more you weigh, the more calories you need/burn per day. This means that as you are losing weight (if weight loss is your goal), you technically burn fewer calories per day, so you will have to adjust your equation every month to make sure you're losing at a consistent rate. You might burn 2,000 calories if you weigh 140 pounds, but as you lose weight the first month and you get down to 136 pounds, you might only naturally burn 1,900 calories. Now eating 1,500 calories a day would only create a 3.5-pound deficit by the end of the month. This is known as **metabolic adaptation**. Your metabolism changes with your body weight. Lighter people burn fewer calories per day and heavier people burn more. If you gain 4 pounds that month, you might burn 2,100 calories instead of 2,000 calories, meaning the following month, you would only gain 3.5 pounds, if that were your goal.

Unit VII. Improving Your Composition: Muscle Gain & Fat Loss (cont.)

If weight loss or gain slows, you should first look and make sure that your activity is staying consistent. As people lose weight, they tend to get slightly lazier. This is their body fighting the weight loss. This can stall weight loss, so it's important to maintain an adequate amount of exercise and physical activity so that the calories you burn per day stays consistent (like walking 10,000 steps per day, every day). You can then adjust your calories monthly to make sure you're losing weight at a consistent pace. Sometimes as you gain weight, you get more energetic and you end up burning the extra calories instead of storing them as weight, so it's equally important to monitor weight gain and change your TDEE calculations to reflect your activity level as discussed in Unit II.

Macronutrients: Your Tools for Body Composition Management

Calories are your tool to increase or decrease weight. **Macronutrient ratios** are your tool for helping make sure that the quality of weight you lose is body fat and the quality of weight you gain is muscle. In Unit III, we learned about protein, carbs, and fats, which are the building blocks, fuel, and support system for your body.

1. **Protein (4 calories/gram):** Builds and repairs muscle, tendon, and ligament tissue like Lego® building blocks, preserves muscle mass during fat loss stages, and supports growth during muscle gain stages.
2. **Carbohydrates (4 calories/gram):** Fuel your workouts and recovery like gasoline for your engine and restock glycogen stores so you can keep strong and energized, and perform at the highest of your athletic ability.
3. **Fats (9 calories/gram):** Support hormones, provide long term energy for low-intensity exercises, and insulate your body and organs to protect against high-impact sports.

Protein is the macronutrient responsible for making sure that any weight you gain is muscle mass and not body fat. By resistance training, we are tearing down our muscles and stimulating growth. By taking in enough dietary protein, we help ensure that we have enough building blocks to rebuild the muscle back bigger and stronger. Carbohydrates fuel the workouts and are typically what get manipulated the most when trying to lose or gain weight. Body fat stays pretty consistent whether your goal is to gain weight or lose weight, as we need just enough to maintain our hormones and essential levels of body fat. For simplicity's sake, protein and fats stay relatively consistent and just depend on body weight and total calories ingested whether you're gaining weight or losing weight. Carbohydrates are the macronutrient that will change the most whether your goal is to lose fat or gain muscle.

Resistance training is the stimulus required to make sure protein gets used to build up skeletal muscle. Without resistance training, taking in excess protein is almost worthless because the extra protein will get converted into glucose and used as energy exactly the same as carbohydrates, except potentially straining the kidneys in the process. As higher protein diets grow in popularity, it's important to note they will only build muscle if you are doing muscle-building exercises. Otherwise, you are potentially wasting the protein.

Unit VII. Improving Your Composition: Muscle Gain & Fat Loss (cont.)

Putting it all Together

Your **TDEE** from Unit II tells you how many calories you burn daily based on your weight and activity level. Using the weight-based rule of thumb (body weight x activity factor), you can estimate your TDEE:

- **Low Activity** (off-season, minimal exercise): 12–14 calories per pound of body weight
- **Moderate Activity** (exercise or sports 3–5 days/week): 15–17 calories per pound of body weight
- **High Activity** (daily intense sports): 18–22 calories per pound of body weight

These numbers will be your baseline to determine your calorie needs. To ensure they are accurate, once you've done your own calculations for your own body weight, track your weight for two weeks. If your weight has stayed consistent (taking a weekly average) from week 1 to week 2, then your calories are balanced and you know you're consuming enough calories to stay the same weight. If you lose weight during this time, then you should increase your calories to the higher end of the equation. If you gain weight, you should move your calories to the lower end of your equation. Retry for another 2 weeks until you reach weight maintenance. From there, you can adjust your calories depending on your goals.

- **Off-Season Muscle Building:** TDEE Maintenance Calories +200 to +300 calories per day
- **Off-Season Fat Loss:** TDEE Maintenance Calories -500 to -750 calories per day

Unfortunately, you can only gain so much muscle per month even with perfect sleep (7–9 hours), great workouts, and a high-protein diet. Only eating in a slight calorie surplus will help make sure that the quality of weight you gain is lean muscle so that you don't have to waste any time in the off-season losing body fat and you can focus on building muscle and practicing skills to improve your athleticism. When you're eating in a surplus, you will have more than enough energy and be in a relatively good mood all the time. When you are in a calorie deficit trying to lose fat, sometimes moodiness increases as well as fatigue and worse athletic performance in the short term because you're not eating as much fuel, constantly having to go into your savings account. For this reason, we want to minimize the amount of fat we gain in the off-season so that it is easy for us to get to our desired body composition for peak in-season performance.

Fortunately, you can lose fat a lot quicker than it takes to gain muscle, and as long as you're eating a high-protein, nutritious diet and resistance training, most of it should be from body fat. For this reason, you can lose 1–1.5 pounds of body fat per week in the off-season, depending on how much you have to lose to get into your desired body composition goal.

Toward the beginning of the off-season, athletes are typically their fittest and leanest coming off of their intense season. It is recommended to immediately go into muscle-building

Unit VII. Improving Your Composition: Muscle Gain & Fat Loss (cont.)

calories and begin resistance training to take advantage of the off-season. As an athlete, keep track of your weight and body fat percent as the off-season goes on. Ideally you should gain 1–2 pounds per month and only see slight increases in your percent body fat. It is normal for percent body fat to be higher than your body fat percentage at the end of the season. In fact, you generally want a little bit of a cushion of body fat reserve at the beginning of your season to act as fuel during your season. You will then slowly start to drop body fat as the season goes on. This is why for every sport and position, you generally have ranges. At the beginning of the season, you might be at the high end of the range, and by the end of the season, you might be at the low end of the range. During the season, it is recommended to eat at maintenance calories.

Macronutrient Ratios

Once you know how many calories you are going to eat depending on your goals, you will need to calculate your **macronutrient ratios**. **Ratio** just means how much (approximately) of each macronutrient you will need to either fuel weight loss or weight gain to help make sure that the quality of weight you gain is muscle and the quality of weight you lose is fat. Think back to previous units on the type of fuel each athlete will use during their sporting activity. This will also help guide you on your macronutrient ratios.

Summary

Losing weight is all about the calorie budget—calories in versus calories out. Losing quality weight or gaining quality muscle, however, is greatly influenced by macronutrient ratios and consistently hitting your protein needs. Find your needs based on your goal and sport. Different sports require nuanced macronutrient ratios, so use the guidelines in previous units and the activity pages to find your own sport and help you, whether your goal is to gain muscle, lose body fat, or maintain what you've got during the season. Remember, you need resistance training as the stimulus to put yourself in a muscle-building mode. The extra protein calories ensure you'll build muscle and not fat. You also need higher protein during fat loss to help make sure you don't lose muscle mass. Athletic performance is the goal here, so don't try to gain or lose weight too quickly. You should only lose 1% of your total body weight per week if that is your goal, and you should aim to gain 1–2 pounds per month if muscle gain is your goal. Consistently track and take a weekly average of your weight and body fat percentage so you know if you're going in the right direction. Manipulate, add, or subtract calories depending on how quickly you're dropping or gaining weight to make sure your focus is always on quality weight loss (body fat loss) and quality weight gain (building muscle mass).

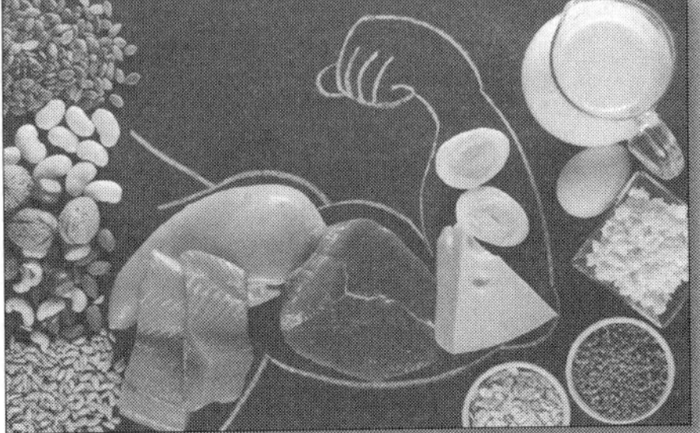

Name: ______________________________ Date: ______________________

Unit VII. Improving Your Composition: Muscle Gain & Fat Loss (cont.)

Activity 10: Practice Calculating Your Calorie and Macronutrient Needs by Energy System

For the first part of the activity, do your own calculations underneath the example for each step of the way. Find out where your calories should be if your goal is to gain muscle or lose fat.

1. **Calculate Your Current Calorie Needs Range**

Step 1: Use the weight-based rule of thumb to calculate your TDEE (body weight x activity factor).

A. **Low Activity** (off season, minimal exercise): 12–14 calories per pound of body weight

B. **Moderate Activity** (exercise or sports 3–5 days per week): 15–17 calories per pound of body weight

C. **High Activity** (daily intense sports or exercise): 18–22 calories per pound of body weight

Example: A 140-pound teen lifting 3x/week (moderate activity) =

Moderate Activity (15–17 calories) x bodyweight (140 pounds)

15 x 140 = 2,100 17 x 140 = 2,380

Calorie Range TDEE: 2,100–2,380 calories/day.

D. **You:** Activity Level ______________ x Bodyweight __________ =

your TDEE ___________________________

Step 2: Choose Your Goal

A. **Fat Loss:** Subtract 500–750 calories per day from your TDEE.

B. **Muscle Gain:** Add 200–300 calories per day to your TDEE.

Example: The 140-pound teen finds he is maintaining his body weight (not gaining and not losing) off 2,100 calories per day (the previous example). He wants to gain muscle in the off season.

TDEE (2,100) + 200 to 300 = Calorie Range of 2,300–2,400

C. **You:** TDEE _________ + Goal: ____________ = Calorie Range ________________

There is a huge difference in weight loss and muscle gain. Remember, never eat below your basal metabolic rate. Even though your calculation might be at the low end of your calories, double check to make sure that isn't below your basal metabolic rate. Slower weight loss results in more muscle preservation, so always start with the most amount of calories you can eat while still losing weight safely. Losing more than 1% of your body weight per week is a sign of malnutrition and can wreak havoc on your health. This means a 150-pound person should never lose more than 1.5 pounds per week. It is important to keep track of your weekly average weight to make sure you're losing fat slowly and preserving your muscle mass.

CD-405099 © Mark Twain Media, Inc., Publishers

Name: ______________________________ Date: ____________________

Unit VII. Improving Your Composition: Muscle Gain & Fat Loss (cont.)

For the second part of the activity, calculate your macronutrient ratios underneath the example for fat loss and muscle gain for each of the energy systems.

2. **Set Your Macronutrient Ratios According to Sport**

   For these calculations, find your TDEE based on your body weight and activity level. Once you have found your TDEE, add 200–300 calories for muscle gain, and then apply the percentages to give you a range of how many calories you need from each macronutrient and how many grams of each macronutrient you need. (Round the grams to the nearest whole number if necessary.) For the fat loss portion, subtract 500 calories from your TDEE since your goal is fat loss, and apply the percentages to again find your calories, protein, carbs, and fats.

   a. **Creatine Phosphate Sports (Weightlifting, Sprinting, Baseball)**
      Muscle Gain:
      - **Protein:** 30–35% (Builds muscle, recommended 0.7–1 g per pound of body weight)
      - **Carbohydrates:** 40–45% (Fuels intense lifts, restocks glycogen)
      - **Fats:** 20–25% (Supports testosterone and estrogen for growth)
      - Example, if someone's TDEE is 2,000 calories and they want to gain muscle, their calorie needs would be 2,200–2,300:
        - Protein: 660–805 calories, or 165–201 g because 4 calories = 1 gram
        - Carbs: 880–1,035 calories, or 220–259 g because 4 calories = 1 gram
        - Fats: 440–575 calories, or 49–64 g because 9 calories = 1 gram

      Based on your calorie needs calculation in the previous section, how many grams of each macronutrient do you need for muscle gain?

      i. Protein: ______________________________
      ii. Carbohydrates: ______________________________
      iii. Fats: ______________________________

      Fat Loss:
      - **Protein:** 35–40% (Builds muscle, recommended 0.8–1 g per pound of body weight)
      - **Carbohydrates:** 35–40% (Fuels intense lifts, restocks glycogen)
      - **Fats:** 20–25% (Supports testosterone and estrogen for growth)
      - Example, if TDEE is 2,000, the fat loss calorie goal would be 1,500:
        - Protein: 525–600 calories, or 131–150 g
        - Carbs: 525–600 calories, or 131–150 g
        - Fats: 300–375 calories, or 33–42 g
      - High protein supports muscle retention. Calories are lowered predominantly from carbs to encourage fat burn.

      Based on your calorie needs calculation in the previous section, how many grams of each macronutrient do you need for fat loss?

      i. Protein: ______________________________
      ii. Carbohydrates: ______________________________
      iii. Fats: ______________________________

CD-405099 © Mark Twain Media, Inc., Publishers

Name: ______________________ Date: ______________

Unit VII. Improving Your Composition: Muscle Gain & Fat Loss (cont.)

b. **Glycolytic Sports (Soccer, Basketball, Wrestling)**
Muscle Gain:

- **Protein:** 25–30% (Builds muscle, recommended 0.7–1 g per pound of body weight)
- **Carbohydrates:** 45–50% (Fuels intense lifts, restocks glycogen)
- **Fats:** 20–25% (Supports testosterone and estrogen for growth)
- Example, if TDEE is 2,000 calories, the goal would be 2,200–2,300 for muscle gain:
  - Protein: 550–690 calories (138–173 g)
  - Carbs: 990–1,150 calories (248–288 g)
  - Fats: 440–575 calories (49–64 g)

Based on your calorie needs calculation in the previous section, how many grams of each macronutrient do you need for muscle gain?

i. Protein: ______________________

ii. Carbohydrates: ______________________

iii. Fats: ______________________

Fat Loss:

- **Protein:** 30–35% (Builds muscle, recommended 0.7–1 g per pound of body weight)
- **Carbohydrates:** 40–45% (Fuels intense lifts, restocks glycogen)
- **Fats:** 20–25% (Supports testosterone and estrogen for growth)
- Example, if TDEE is 2,000, the calorie goal would be 1,500 for fat loss:
  - Protein: 450–525 calories (113–131 g)
  - Carbs: 600–675 calories (150–169 g)
  - Fats: 300–375 calories (33–42 g)
- Higher carbs support intense training sessions, slightly lower for fat loss. Protein ensures muscle repair and retention.

Based on your calorie needs calculation in the previous section, how many grams of each macronutrient do you need for fat loss?

i. Protein: ______________________

ii. Carbohydrates: ______________________

iii. Fats: ______________________

CD-405099 © Mark Twain Media, Inc., Publishers

Name: ______________________ Date: ______________

Unit VII. Improving Your Composition: Muscle Gain & Fat Loss (cont.)

c. **Oxidative Sports (Cross Country, Swimming, Distance Cycling)**
Muscle Gain:

- **Protein:** 20–25% (Muscle repair)
- **Carbohydrates:** 50–55% (Fuels endurance and glycogen stores)
- **Fats:** 20–25% (Supports testosterone and estrogen for growth)
- Example, if your TDEE is 2,000, your calorie goal would be 2,200–2,300 per day for muscle gain:
  - ❍ Protein: 440–575 calories (110–144 g)
  - ❍ Carbs: 1,100–1,265 calories (275–316 g)
  - ❍ Fats: 440–575 calories (49–64 g)

Based on your calorie needs calculation in the previous section, how many grams of each macronutrient do you need for muscle gain?

i. Protein: ______________________

ii. Carbohydrates: ______________________

iii. Fats: ______________________

Fat Loss:

- **Protein:** 25–30% (Muscle maintenance)
- **Carbohydrates:** 45–50% (Fuels intense lifts, restocks glycogen)
- **Fats:** 20–25% (Supports testosterone and estrogen for growth)
- Example, if your TDEE is 2,000, your calorie goal would be 1,500 per day for fat loss:
  - ❍ Protein: 375–450 calories (94–113 g)
  - ❍ Carbs: 675–750 calories (169–188 g)
  - ❍ Fats: 300–375 calories (33–42 g)
- High carbs fuel longer sessions, slightly lower for fat loss. Protein supports recovery or preservation, and fats aid endurance and health.

Based on your calorie needs calculation in the previous section, how many grams of each macronutrient do you need for fat loss?

i. Protein: ______________________

ii. Carbohydrates: ______________________

iii. Fats: ______________________

Unit VIII. Pre-/Intra-/Post-Workout Nutrition & Hydration

Pre-/Intra-/Post-Workout Nutrition Overview

The last unit talked about how to safely lose fat and gain muscle. It went over the macronutrient ratios to help maximize muscle gain and minimize fat gain when gaining muscle, and how to maximize fat loss and minimize muscle loss when losing weight. It emphasized maintaining performance in the off-season and continually improving each year. Weight management over the course of the year, to improve your performance long term, is like looking at the overall big picture, or **macro level**, of your nutritional performance. Your day-to-day activities and workouts, however, are like taking a magnifying glass to the macro scale and focusing on the **micro nutritional details** of each and every practice, workout, and game, and initiating the recovery process after to help make sure you continue performing your best throughout the year and season. The micro level of your nutrition is known as your **pre-/intra-/post-workout nutrition** and takes into consideration your carbohydrates for immediate fuel and your protein to initiate the recovery process. This concept also introduces hydration tactics to make sure you stay hydrated despite losing a lot of water and electrolytes to keep you performing your best during the workout, practice, or game.

- **Pre-** = Before
- **Intra-** = During
- **Post-** = After

Why Timing Matters

Your body's three energy systems, or motors, need to be fueled at specific times. A volleyball spike uses the creatine phosphate system and creatine as fuel for quick power. A soccer fast break taps into the glycolytic system and uses quick and fast glucose and glycogen in your bloodstream (blood sugar) to fuel its speed down the field. A cross country run leans heavily on stored glycogen and stored body fat as fuel for endurance. On top of different energy needs, you can lose 1–3 liters of sweat per hour, which is packed with **electrolytes** like sodium, chloride, potassium, magnesium, and calcium. Electrolytes have a natural electric charge when dissolved in water. Replacing water and electrolytes is crucial to avoid fatigue and cramps during activity and kickstart the recovery process so you don't feel tired and depleted the rest of the day. We'll cover how to nail your nutrition on the micro scale and how to strategically use protein to start your body's regeneration and muscle-building response, along with avoiding breaking down muscle during your intense workouts.

Pre-Workout Nutrition: Charge Your Engine

Pre-workout nutrition focuses on ensuring you have optimal energy, fueled by carbohydrates, to perform your best and decrease the risk of breaking down your own muscle mass for energy. In order to do this, your pre-workout nutrition will focus on two strategies. Choosing which strategy comes down to how long you have before the game or practice. A heavy meal 30 minutes before the game will leave you feeling tired and sluggish and might end up on the field or court after you throw up. Too light of a meal, however, and you could tire down quicker and perform suboptimally.

1. **Full Meal:** A full meal should be eaten 2–3 hours before the game, practice, or workout. Complex carbohydrates should be prioritized since you won't need to use the glucose for a few hours.

Unit VIII. Pre-/Intra-/Post-Workout Nutrition & Hydration (cont.)

2. **Snack:** If you only have time for a snack, you should still consume pre-workout carbohydrates but in simple form, focusing on fruit, honey, or in a pinch, candy, because it is very quickly broken down and used for energy.

What to Eat:

- **Carbohydrates:** Shoot for 30–50 g (120–200 calories) of carbs before your workout or game.
  - Simple Carbs: 2 slices of white bread, 2 tablespoons of honey, 1.5 cups of fruit juice, 2 medium bananas, 2.5 cups of pineapple, or 2 apples
  - Complex Carbs: 1 cup of brown rice, 1.5 cups of quinoa, 1.5 cups of oatmeal, 1 cup of whole wheat pasta, or 1 sweet potato
- **Protein:** Aim for 20 g (80 calories) to support muscle repair and prevent muscle breakdown during exercise.
  - 3 oz. chicken breast, 1 cup of egg whites, ¾ cup of Greek yogurt, ¾ cup cottage cheese, 4 oz. white fish, 1 cup tofu, or 1 scoop of protein powder
- **Fat:** Keep fat relatively low since fat is too slow-digesting and can weigh down your stomach before a game.

Intra-Workout Nutrition: Keeping the Tank Full and Hydrated

During long or intense games, workouts, or practices, you'll have to keep your tank from running dry. Intra- (during) nutrition will focus on replacing any carbohydrates and electrolytes lost in sweat and work to maintain energy and prevent cramping, especially in hot environments. Sip or snack every 15–20 minutes, and any water you consume should be electrolyte-enriched containing sodium, potassium, magnesium, and chloride. A popular supplement, called **BCAA (branch chain amino acids)** is marketed as an intra-workout protein supplement to help keep your body from breaking down muscle mass. Many of these supplements will also contain electrolytes for the same cost, as it protects muscle mass and also fights against dehydration.

What to Drink:

- **Carbs:** Aim for 15–30 g of simple carbs per hour (like a sports drink, gel, or juice) to keep blood sugar steady.
- **Electrolytes:** Replace sodium, potassium, magnesium, and chloride with an electrolyte mix. Water down the mix to the ratio that tastes slightly salty. As a general rule of thumb, if you can't taste the salt, then there's not enough sodium in it to replace your electrolytes. ***Fun fact: If you're always craving fast food, chips, or fries after a workout, it is a sign that your body is screaming for electrolytes, especially sodium. Fuel up with electrolytes to keep your calories down and to keep from eating processed foods after the game.***
- **Protein:** Skip regular protein because it digests too slowly to help with activity. You can, however, supplement BCAA or EAA (essential amino acids) as they are already broken down protein molecules, and your body can use them quicker than regular protein. Find a brand of electrolytes that also has BCAA or EAA in them.
- **Fats:** Avoid fats during activity. They are heavy on the stomach and too slow-digesting to help in performance.

Unit VIII. Pre-/Intra-/Post-Workout Nutrition & Hydration (cont.)

Post-Workout Nutrition: Rebuild and Refuel

The goal of the post-workout is to refill your gas tank and also start the repair/regeneration process known as **muscle protein synthesis**. Quick carbs after a workout spike your insulin levels, which helps shuttle protein to your muscles to start the repair process. Chocolate milk with some added protein (roughly 25–30 g total) is the king of recovery drinks because it has just enough sugar to start the regeneration process and just enough protein to help turn it all into muscle.

What to Eat:

- **Protein:** Aim for 25–30 g of protein to jumpstart muscle repair and prevent breakdown. Any protein supplementation should contain around 2.5 g of **leucine**, the key amino acid responsible for stimulating the regrowth/regeneration inside the muscle.
- **Carbs:** Shoot for 60–90 g (usually 2–3x protein grams) to help refuel glycogen storage. Simple carbohydrates should be prioritized here, but any carbohydrate will do.
- **Fats:** Keep fats to a minimum; they are too slow-digesting and will slow down the digestion process, inhibiting muscle protein synthesis. You don't have to skip family dinner just because you want to keep your fats low. Any of these goals should be sustainable and built around your own life.
- **Hydration:** Drink 20–24 oz. of water per pound of body weight lost during the game/practice. This is another good time for a hydration packet to quickly refuel your electrolytes and get rid of any fatigue, lethargy, or post-workout cramps associated with dehydration.

Creatine Supplementation

Creatine is the only fuel that takes weeks to build up in the system for any benefits. Remember, this is the energy system you will use for your quick and explosive movements. It is found in meat and fish, but also incredibly cheap and easy to supplement. 5 grams is the recommended dosage per day if you choose to supplement. It will take several weeks to fully "fill" that gas tank or energy system. When you initially start supplementing, you'll naturally be thirstier and gain several pounds of extra water weight that will actually aid in your overall hydration levels. Creatine has been shown to help sports performance, mental health, bone density, disease prevention, and is quickly growing in studies and popularity as an anti-aging supplement as well as a top-tier level supplement for enhanced performance. Always clear any supplementation with your parents and consult a physician to determine if this is a healthy solution for you.

Summary

Don't over stress about making every workout or practice perfect when it comes to eating. Ultimately, find what works for you through experimentation in the practices and workouts. That way, you know exactly what works for your body when it counts in season during the actual games. If you know you suffer from dehydration symptoms, pack extra electrolytes during practice and try to gauge how many you need to perform your best. If you digest food slowly, try eating 3–4 hours before instead of 2–3. You might feel better with some fruit over complex carbs if you have to have a snack instead of a full meal. Journal what foods sit well with you and what you seem to recover with the best. This will help you perform your best and prevent dehydration, which can lead to serious injuries.

Name: ______________________________ Date: ______________________

Unit VIII. Pre-/Intra-/Post-Workout Nutrition & Hydration (cont.)

Activity 11: Nutrition & Hydration Word Unscramble

Below are sports nutrition terms that need to be unscrambled. Rearrange the letters to reveal the correct spelling.

1. TENPROI ______________________
2. RINTYHOAD ______________________
3. OAMRC ______________________
4. COYLEESTRTEL ______________________
5. ORK-OTUPERW ______________________
6. TCEEINRA ______________________
7. PWOS-OTROUKT ______________________
8. ARLCOIE URUSPLS ______________________
9. STFA ______________________
10. NIAOM SDIAC ______________________
11. PENTSATONILUPEM ______________________
12. EBOHRACYATRD ______________________
13. TOUI-KNRTORWA ______________________
14. CIMOR ______________________
15. EALIORC FIDECIT ______________________

Activity 12: Comparing Electrolytes

Research two types of sports drinks and two types of hydration packets to analyze the electrolytes and other macro and micronutrients included. You can either visit a grocery store or nutrition store or research the products online.

On your own paper, make a chart comparing the two sports drinks and the two nutrition packets. List all the ingredients and the calories of each product. Which product or products do you think would provide the most benefit to boost hydration and replenish nutrients after a game or workout?

Unit IX. Special Diet Considerations

Special Diet Considerations Overview

Special diet considerations take into account the current and growing trends in the nutritional world as well as allergies and intolerances. **Gluten intolerances, seafood, nut, milk, and egg allergies** are some of the most common in the world. Lifestyle changes and special diets also influence how people eat and include **low carb** (keto/carnivore) diets, **plant-based** (vegan/vegetarian) diets, and even timing of when you can eat and when you can't eat (mimicking fasting), called **intermittent fasting**. This chapter will help you navigate the pros and cons of these diet considerations.

Allergies

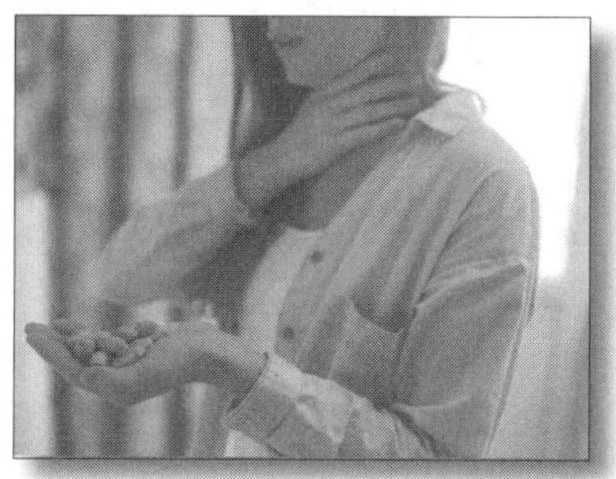

Food allergies are sensitivities to food or ingredients that trigger an immune system reaction within the body that can create itching, hives, and **anaphylaxis** (breathing airway obstruction) and can lead to death. Mild allergies can go unknown for years while the more severe allergies are typically caught early in life. Emergency treatment for an allergic reaction can involve injecting epinephrine with an EpiPen®, which is a prescription medicine you should carry with you at all times if you are allergic to any foods.

The nine biggest allergies affecting 8% of children globally are **milk, eggs, peanuts, tree nuts, fish, crustacean shellfish, wheat (gluten), soy, and sesame**. Whether allergies are growing in prevalence or we have better diagnostic tools, it is recommended to get allergy tested early on so you know what foods you can eat and what foods to avoid. This will help you navigate your eating choices to gain weight, lose fat, and fuel your workouts, practices, and games.

For instance, if you're **lactose intolerant**, you might not be able to use milk in your post-workout to initiate the recovery process. Luckily, **whey isolate protein powder** is highly filtered. The majority, if not all, of the lactose has been filtered out, making it a great choice for someone who typically can't handle lactose. Different sources of protein powder, including **brown rice/pea protein powder, animal-based protein powder, and soy protein powder**, are all great alternatives as long as it has around 2.5 grams of leucine within the serving size. Look for lactose-free milks and dairy free on the back of any nutritional label.

If you are allergic to **shellfish or fish**, this cuts out many sources of protein and omega-3s. To combat this, you would have to eat other protein sources and possibly supplement algae oil to help get enough **omega-3 fatty acids** (highly anti-inflammatory and good for the heart, brain, and muscle building). Be sure to check the nutrition label of foods. Sometimes shellfish or fish ingredients are used in foods you may not realize would have shellfish or fish in them.

If you are allergic to **peanuts and tree nuts**, not only will you have to eliminate this food group and find alternative fat sources, you will also need to check the back of every label of food that you plan on eating. There are many unexpected sources of nuts in processed or packaged foods, such as peanut oil or almond paste, so always look for the allergen warning on the back of the nutrition label.

If you are allergic to **wheat, eggs, soy, or sesame**, you will also have to check the back of every nutrition label. Luckily, there are many gluten-free flours that taste very similar to the real deal, and you can generally find gluten-free alternatives in health markets. If you're allergic

Unit IX. Special Diet Considerations (cont.)

to soy and sesame, you may need to stay away from Asian food and sauces for good. Soy ingredients are found in a wide variety of foods so always be careful.

On food nutrition labels, the ingredients and allergen statements are listed underneath all the macronutrient and micronutrient information. There, you will find information regarding any of these common allergens. It is illegal not to disclose this information on the label, so always double check. Sometimes you see phrases like "produced in a factory that contains wheat." In those situations, they're letting you know that the food could be **cross-contaminated** even if it doesn't directly have that allergen within the food. Always avoid cross-contamination by staying away from these foods, using separate utensils from your friends, staying away from kitchens that contain these foods, and making separate dishes. Even small particles can cause a severe reaction.

Low Carb Diets

Low carb diets, such as **ketogenic** (keto) or **carnivore diets** (eating only meat), heavily restrict carbohydrate intake. These diets typically only allow 20–50 grams per day in order to keep the body in **ketosis**, burning fat as fuel for energy. By eliminating an entire macronutrient food group, it is easier to stay in a calorie deficit and get adequate amounts of protein to maintain muscle mass. While keto restricts carbohydrates, carnivore diets only allow meat, fish, eggs, and sometimes dairy. Both diets aim to reduce insulin and blood sugar spikes, promote fat loss, and stabilize energy levels, but they pose some major disadvantages for athletes.

- **Pros:**
  - May aid in fat loss by creating a calorie deficit due to high fullness (satiety).
  - Helps stabilize blood sugar, reducing energy crashes for the general population whose general activities are low in intensity.
  - Carnivore diets may simplify eating rather than keeping track of calories.
- **Cons:**
  - Restricting carbohydrates deprives the body of its most useful fuel for moderate- to high-intensity activities and can lower sports performance in season.
  - Low carb diets reduce glycogen stores, which often leads to fatigue, reduces power output, and slows recovery after workouts. The body also sheds a lot of water, which is seen by the drastic weight loss within the first week of starting a low carb diet. This can result in dehydration and worsening sports performance.
  - Limited fruit and vegetable intake can lead to fiber, vitamin C, and potassium deficiencies, impacting gut health, the immune system, electrolyte balance, and recovery.
  - Hormonal health can be disrupted, especially for women and in growing teens as carbs support testosterone and estrogen production.
- **Strategies for Athletes:**
  - Prioritize nutrient-dense carbohydrate foods like fruit before your workout to help immediately fuel your workout or game, and keep simple carbohydrates on hand in case you need to refuel intra-workout.

Unit IX. Special Diet Considerations (cont.)

- Time 20–30 g of pre-workout carbs before any exercise, training, or game.
- Load up on low-calorie green vegetables to maintain fiber levels for gut health.
- Supplement with electrolytes (sodium, potassium, magnesium, chloride) to replace lower levels of hydration and water loss.
- Consult with a dietitian to ensure adequate micronutrient intake.
- Use as a weight-loss strategy during the off-season. In season, increase carbohydrate intake to match your activity level.

Plant-Based Diets (Vegan/Vegetarian)

Vegan and vegetarian diets prioritize **plant-based** products and widely exclude animal products. **Vegetarian diets** allow for dairy and/or eggs, but **vegan diets** exclude any product that contains any animal content. These diets are popularized for their ethical, environmental, and cardiovascular health benefits. However, it requires planning for athletes to meet their high-performance needs, especially since it becomes very difficult to get usable protein to repair and build muscle mass and recovery.

- **Pros:**
  - High in fiber, phytonutrients, and antioxidants from fruits, vegetables, and grains, supporting recovery and reducing inflammation.
  - Lower in saturated fat, which can lead to a healthier circulatory system for endurance sports.
  - Can support weight management and weight loss due to the low-calorie, high-nutrient density of plant-based foods.
- **Cons:**
  - Risk of major deficiencies in protein, omega-3 fatty acids, iron, zinc, vitamin B12, and vitamin D, which are crucial for muscle repair, oxygen transport, and energy, especially for females with an ovulation cycle who risk anemic (low iron) deficiencies anyway.
  - Plant-based proteins (beans, lentils, peas, soy) are less bioavailable and may lack the essential amino acids to build muscle, so steps must be taken to pair incomplete proteins together to help form complete proteins (e.g., rice and beans).
  - High fiber intake can cause bloating or digestive discomfort during intense workouts.
- **Strategies for Athletes:**
  - Eat a wide variety of plant proteins to make sure you're getting all the essential amino acids to build and repair muscle, tendons, ligaments, and cartilage.
  - Supplement vitamin B12 and consider algae-based supplements for omega-3s.
  - Eat iron-rich foods, such as spinach and lentils, with vitamin C-rich foods to enhance absorption of iron to prevent anemic symptoms during menstruation.
  - Monitor energy and recovery. If performance suffers, consult a dietitian to adjust protein intake and consider switching from vegan to the less exclusionary vegetarian or **pescatarian** (vegetarian but can still eat fish) lifestyle.

Unit IX. Special Diet Considerations (cont.)

Intermittent Fasting (IF)

Intermittent fasting involves cycling between eating and **fasting** (not eating) periods. Intermittent fasting protocols range from 16:8 (16 hours fasting, 8-hour eating window) all the way up to 20:4 (20 hours fasting, 4-hour eating window) warrior fasts. This strategy is popular for its weight-management benefits. By restricting the hours that you can eat, you greatly limit the amount of food and calories you can eat because your stomach fills up so fast. This is even more apparent with whole foods, which take longer to digest than processed foods, making you fill up very quickly and making it very difficult to get calories in if weight gain is your goal.

- **Pros:**
  - ❍ May promote fat loss by creating a calorie deficit.
  - ❍ Can simplify meal planning by reducing the eating window.
  - ❍ Can improve blood sugar sensitivity and reduce systemic inflammation.
- **Cons:**
  - ❍ Can deplete glycogen stores, reducing energy for high-intensity workouts.
  - ❍ Limited eating windows can make it hard to consume enough calories and protein to repair muscle, promote recovery, and gain muscle and strength.
  - ❍ There is a risk of overeating on low-quality food because hunger is so great, it can lead to disordered eating like binge eating.
  - ❍ May lower testosterone and estrogen if calories are too low for too long. Not advised for female athletes at all on a monthly hormone cycle.
- **Strategies for Athletes:**
  - ❍ Schedule workouts during or just before the eating window to ensure you've had simple carbohydrates pre-workout to help fuel your workout, eating your largest carbohydrate and protein meal directly after the workout.
  - ❍ Make sure to break the fast with whole foods, specifically protein and fats, to help kickstart recovery, prevent cycles of carbohydrate binges, and maximize micronutrient and fiber intake in fewer meals.
  - ❍ Avoid fasting on game days or intense workout days.
  - ❍ Monitor energy, mood, and performance. If a drop in performance occurs, consider shortening your fast or contact a dietitian to help navigate your diet.

Summary

Special diets are not typically recommended for growing teenagers. Heavy restriction of any kind can lead to disordered eating or negative beliefs about the self, body image, or foods. Special planning and consideration must be taken if any of these diet strategies are utilized for whatever reason to ensure that you don't become deficient in any nutrients crucial for growth and development. Allergies must be managed by reading labels and finding safe alternatives. Low carb diets may hinder sports performance, and carbohydrates will have to be timed strategically to offset this. Plant-based diets will need to prioritize complete protein intake, vitamin B12 supplementation, and omega-3 fatty acids. Intermittent fasting can be difficult to prioritize nutrient timing so training doesn't suffer. As always, get to know your body—if energy, recovery, or performance suffer, adjust your approach with the help of a registered dietitian.

Unit X. Supplementation

Supplementation Overview

Supplements are tools to fill nutritional gaps in a teen athlete's diet, especially when whole foods alone can't meet the high demands of growth, training, and performance. Sometimes whole foods can present a financial barrier. For example, if you're someone who struggles with an iron deficiency (especially females menstruating) and feels great eating red meat, that meat can increase the grocery bill and be hard to afford to eat consistently. Protein, unfortunately, being the most important macronutrient for recovery and growth development, is also the most costly per serving. Carbohydrates and fat, in comparison, are much cheaper. Foods like rice, oats, and even quinoa are very inexpensive carbohydrate sources. Oils are also very inexpensive and easy to load up on to get sources of fat. For this reason, sometimes supplementing gaps in nutrition is less expensive and easier to do, which is why the supplement industry has grown so much in recent years, becoming a multi-billion-dollar industry.

For high school athletes, the focus of this book will be on safe, effective, evidence-based supplements that enhance performance on and off the field while also supporting overall health. This unit will cover key supplements—**whey protein, creatine, electrolytes, and multivitamins**—explaining their roles, benefits, and how they address dietary shortfalls. For those who prefer not to supplement, practical food alternatives will be provided to achieve similar benefits. The goal is to empower athletes to make informed choices. Many supplement marketing strategies make very hefty promises for increased performance. We will focus on time-tested, safe supplements to enhance performance, recovery, energy, and resilience.

Whey Protein Isolate

Whey protein isolate is a fast-digesting, high-quality protein source rich in all the essential amino acids needed to trigger muscle protein synthesis and immediately begin the recovery process after a hard workout or game. Whey protein isolate is a milk product that has been filtered so many times to capture the protein that it has also lost most, if not all, of its **lactose**, making it a lactose-free product. This is great for those athletes who are lactose intolerant or are worried about lactose-induced skin issues. Whey isolate has already filtered out all of the lactose, making it safe for lactose intolerant athletes. It will support muscle repair and growth and prevent muscle breakdown in times of intense effort or calorie restriction. It is essential to keep protein high in and off season to maintain muscle mass, which makes this a very useful tool for athletes who struggle to eat enough protein through whole foods due to busy schedules or very high caloric needs. Whey protein isolate is $1–$2 per serving, making it very cheap compared to chicken, beef, or pork protein, which can cost anywhere from $3–$10 per serving.

Benefits:

- Boosts muscle recovery after resistance training, practice, and games. Reduces soreness and improves readiness for the next session, allowing the athlete to get more done per week without risk of overtraining or injury.
- Helps speed up healing and prevent minor injuries and overuse injuries. Tendons, ligaments, and cartilage are all made up of essential amino acids, all found in whey protein. This means supplementation will also help soft tissue recovery just as much as muscle recovery.

Unit X. Supplementation (cont.)

- Helps meet daily protein needs for muscle maintenance or growth. This helps build muscle in the off season, maintain muscle during season, and prevent muscle tissue breakdown when dieting or in a calorie deficit to optimize performance within a weight class.
- Convenient and easy to digest for post-workout nutrition when whole food meals aren't immediately available, like after a game or practice when the next meal still might be an hour or two away.

Usage as a Tool:

- Take 20–30 g within 30 minutes post workout to kickstart recovery, paired with 60–90 g of carbohydrates (like chocolate milk or fruit).
- Use it as a snack in between meals to hit daily protein targets or to keep you full during periods of weight loss/calorie restriction.
- Normal whey protein concentrate can be used for people who aren't lactose sensitive, but whey protein isolate should be used for lactose intolerant athletes to minimize lactose issues.

Food Alternatives:

- **Chocolate Milk:** 3 cups of chocolate milk contains 24 g of protein. Brands like Fairlife® are also lactose free and contain more protein per serving, with 3 cups being close to 39 g of protein. Chocolate milk also contains fast-digesting carbohydrates to quickly restore and refill glycogen stores.
- **Greek Yogurt:** 1.5 cups of plain Greek yogurt offers 30–40 g protein. Add fruit to increase the amount of carbohydrates to help replenish glycogen after a workout.

- **Chicken Breast:** 3 oz. of cooked chicken is anywhere from 20–24 g of protein. Add white or jasmine rice to increase carbohydrates to refill glycogen.
- **Eggs:** 4 whole eggs is 24 g of protein. Pair this with some waffles, hash browns, or roasted potatoes to get your protein and carbohydrates in right after a workout.
- **Cottage Cheese:** 1 cup of low-fat cottage cheese has around 20 g of protein. Pair with pineapple, peaches, or other fruit to increase carbohydrate intake to refill glycogen storage.

Caution: Not all protein shakes are created equally. Look for third-party or banned substance tested formulas to make sure you are getting exactly what you need. Look for high leucine (2–3 g) protein formulas to make sure you're getting enough leucine to stimulate protein synthesis. If totally lactose free, look for vegan/vegetarian options in pea/brown rice formulas, keeping a close eye on leucine content to make sure your body can use it for muscle building. Protein shakes should be used in addition to your regular diet, not to replace meals on a regular basis. Most protein formulas don't have fiber or micronutrients, making it a poor choice to get your vitamins and minerals.

Unit X. Supplementation (cont.)

Creatine Monohydrate

Creatine's role in performance fuels the ATP-PC (creatine) energy system, which provides the body with powerful short, explosive energy required for sprinting, throwing, jumping, hitting, or lifting. For teen athletes, this aids in hydration, enhances strength and power, and improves muscular endurance. Sports like baseball, volleyball, weightlifting, dance, wrestling, and track will see the most notable differences.

Benefits:

- Increases power output for high-intensity efforts (soccer sprint or basketball dunk).
- Enhances muscle growth by improving workout capacity and recovery, retaining more glycogen inside muscles.
- Improves cognition and helps with focus during games or practices; also excellent for recovery after concussions.
- Safe and well studied for teens who have healthy kidneys, with benefits going far beyond sports performance.

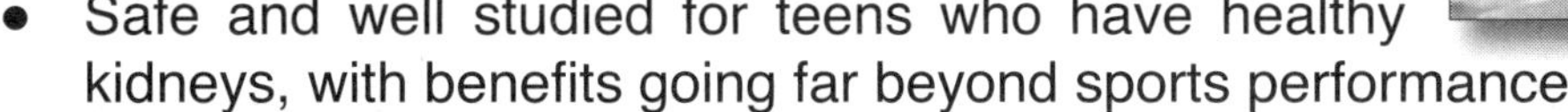

Usage as a Tool:

- Take 5 g daily mixed with water, juice, or a protein shake any time of day. It takes several weeks to fully fill up energy storage, so time of day doesn't matter.
- No need for the loading phase (10–20 g/day) as this can cause an upset stomach and bloating.
- Stay hydrated and try to drink extra water the first couple of weeks. Creatine monohydrate draws water into muscles, which can lead to dehydration everywhere else if you're not consuming enough water.
- Use consistently to keep muscles fully saturated. There is no need to cycle off and on, as this will just decrease performance only to increase it again later.

Food Alternatives:

- **Steak:** 1 lb. cooked beef provides 4–5 g of creatine and could be split up between meals in a day or in conjunction with other food sources to get a day full of creatine.
- **Salmon:** 1 lb. cooked salmon provides around 4 g of creatine and could be split up between meals or used with other food sources to get a full day's worth.
- **Pork:** 1 lb. cooked pork yields 3–4 g creatine and could be used in conjunction with other food sources to get an adequate amount of creatine per day.

Caution: Clear with a physician before starting, especially if you have kidney concerns. Creatine will cause an initial weight gain of 2–4 pounds, which is normal and a part of the hydration process that increases sports performance.

Electrolytes

Electrolytes (sodium, potassium, magnesium, chloride, and calcium) regulate fluid balance inside and outside of the cells in your body. This causes muscle contractions and provides nerve signals to the muscles that allow our bodies to work and play sports. When

Unit X. Supplementation (cont.)

we're low on electrolytes, our nerve signals are slower and our muscles' ability to contract properly decreases, which worsens performance and increases the odds of cramps, injuries, and fatigue—this is known as **dehydration**. Supplementing electrolytes during practice, games, or intense workout sessions maintains performance and hydration, and is crucial during hot weather or long practices to keep performance running well.

Benefits:

- Prevents muscle cramps and dizziness during games, especially in hot weather or double headers.
- Sustains endurance by maintaining hydration and muscle function.
- Speeds up recovery by replacing minerals lost in sweat, reducing post-workout fatigue for the day.
- Used whenever an athlete is sweating a lot, even if it doesn't have to do with sports performance. Mowing the lawn on a hot summer day is a great time to drink some electrolytes and water to minimize fatigue for practice later that day.
- Reduces cravings for salty food post workout, which helps support healthier eating habits and makes it easier to stay on track with caloric restriction during periods of weight loss.

Usage as a Tool:

- Mix an electrolyte packet (containing 500–1,000 mg of sodium, 200–400 mg of potassium, 50–100 mg of magnesium) into 16–20 oz. of water and sip throughout workouts or games.
- Choose zero-calorie options to avoid excess sugar unless you are using the sugar as a tool to increase performance intra workout.
- Add a packet to 20–24 oz. water to replace sweat loss after a workout, game, or sauna session.
- Adjust based on sweat rate and cravings. If you're craving salty foods after a workout, game, or practice, chances are you aren't replacing your electrolytes appropriately. If done correctly, you won't cramp during games, and performance will not falter even during hot weather.

Food Alternatives:

- Pickles: 1 large dill pickle provides 800 mg of sodium.
- Olives: 10 large olives offer 400 mg of sodium.
- Celery: 2 stalks with a salt sprinkle yield 100 mg of sodium and 50 mg of potassium.
- Bananas: 1 medium banana has 400 mg of potassium.

Caution: Overloading sodium without actually sweating that much can cause water retention and stress on your kidneys trying to urinate all of the extra electrolytes. If you aren't moving a lot or sweating a lot, general water and electrolytes found in your normal diet will be sufficient to keep you hydrated. Electrolyte packets are to be used strategically during times of intense heat, sweat, or hard work.

Unit X. Supplementation (cont.)

Multivitamins

Multivitamins offer a broad spectrum of micronutrients (vitamins A, B, C, D, E, and K, and minerals like zinc, iron, and magnesium) to fill the gaps in your diet. Athletes with high metabolisms and high-energy demands with picky eating habits have a hard time getting all the essential nutrients from diet alone, making multivitamins a standard in the morning rituals. They help support energy, production, immune health, muscle repair, and ensure consistent performance. As always, athletes should prioritize whole food diets and eat a large variety of foods to help ensure micronutrients are covered as well as macronutrients. A good multivitamin will give you a headstart every morning to help reach your micronutrient quota for the day.

Benefits:

- Boosts immune function to reduce sick days and risk of overtraining in athletes (specifically vitamin C and zinc).
- Supports energy metabolism for endurance and focus (B vitamins and iron).
- Enhances recovery by aiding in bone and muscle development (magnesium, calcium, and vitamin D).
- Supports hormone production (zinc, selenium, magnesium, and iron).

Usage as a Tool:

- Take 1 daily multivitamin with a fat and protein-heavy meal (typically breakfast) to enhance absorption and avoid an upset stomach.
- For teens, choose a formula with 50–100% Daily Value (DV) on the back of the label for most nutrients to avoid overdosing. Many minerals compete for absorption, so your body will not be able to use everything you intake with the multivitamin right away. Many vitamins and minerals are water soluble so you will simply urinate out whatever your body doesn't need. This makes the risk of overdosing very low on multivitamins.
- Once started, it is recommended to take regular blood tests with the help of your physician or dietitian to see what you're deficient in before adding any more individual vitamins or minerals.

Food Alternatives:

- **Beef Liver:** 3 oz. provides vitamin A, B12, iron, zinc, and more micronutrients.
- **Salmon:** 4 oz. offers vitamin D, B vitamins, selenium, and healthy omega-3 fatty acids.
- **Spinach:** 2 cups raw spinach with bell peppers contain vitamin C, folate, and magnesium.
- **Eggs:** 2 large eggs supply vitamin B, vitamin D, and choline.
- **Mixed Berries:** 1 cup of mixed berries provides vitamin C, antioxidants, and anti-aging phytonutrients.

Caution: Avoid high doses of multivitamins (greater than 200% DV), as fat-soluble vitamins (vitamins A, D, E, K) can accumulate quickly and cause toxicity.

Name: ______________________________ Date: ______________________

Unit X. Supplementation (cont.)

Activity 13: Supplement Match-Up

Draw lines to match the supplement with its main benefit and then find its whole food alternative.

Whey Protein	A. Boosts explosive power	1. Beef Liver
Creatine	B. Supports muscle repair	2. Chocolate Milk
Electrolytes	C. Maintains hydration	3. Steak
Multivitamin	D. Micronutrients	4. Pickles

Activity 14: Supplement Fill-in-the-Blank

Fill in the blank in each statement with a term from the Supplementation unit.

1. Creatine monohydrate can improve ______________ and help with focus during games or practices.
2. ______________ is the most expensive macronutrient per serving.
3. ______________ can prevent muscle cramps and dizziness during games.
4. Micronutrients found in ______________ can boost immune functions, support metabolism, enhance recovery, and support hormone production.
5. Whey protein isolate is a milk product that has been filtered so many times it is considered ______________ free.
6. It is recommended to have regular ______________ ______________ to see which vitamins or minerals you might be deficient in.

Unit XI. Conclusion: Fueling Your Sport

Sports Nutrition for Teenagers has equipped you with the tools to optimize your athletic performance through informed nutritional choices. It is a comprehensive guide to fueling your body so that you can apply these principles not only to your athletic journey, but to the rest of your life, maintaining a fit and healthy lifestyle and reaching your body composition goals.

Key Highlights

1. **Nutrition as Fuel for Performance:** Your body is a remarkable machine that requires the right fuel to excel in your given sport. Your body heavily relies on calories and macronutrients to fuel your sports and optimize your recovery. Proper nutrition not only boosts physical performance but also your mental health, growth, and recovery.
2. **Calorie Management and Body Composition:**
   a. **Calorie Deficit:** Consistently eating fewer calories than your Total Daily Energy Expenditure (TDEE) leads to weight loss. When paired with a high-protein diet and resistance training, the quality of weight you will lose will be mostly body fat. A 500–750 calorie deficit per day can result in 1–1.5 pounds of fat loss per week. Never eat below your Basal Metabolic Rate (BMR) to avoid health risks.
   b. **Calorie Surplus:** Eating more calories than your TDEE supports weight gain, and by resistance training and eating a high-protein diet, the majority of the weight should be lean body mass (muscle). Choose a modest surplus of 200–300 calories per day to try to gain 1–2 pounds of muscle per week to help minimize fat gain.
3. **Macronutrients for Optimal Performance:**
   a. **Protein:** Essential for muscle repair, growth, and recovery. Aim for 0.7–1 g per pound of body weight daily, especially for sports requiring strength and frequent training. High-protein diets preserve muscle during fat loss stages and maximize muscle gains during muscle building stages.
   b. **Carbohydrates:** The body's preferred energy source, critical for fueling moderate to high-intensity activities. Simple carbs provide quick energy, while complex carbs sustain energy for longer periods of time. Athletes in glycolytic or oxidative sports should prioritize higher carb intakes to maximize athletic performance.
   c. **Fats:** Support hormone production, long-term energy, and maintain cell health. Make sure 20–25% of your total calories come from fat, favoring unsaturated fats like olive oil, fish, or nuts for anti-inflammation, brain function, and recovery.
4. **Pre-/Intra-/Post-Workout Nutrition for Peak Performance:**
   a. **Pre-Workout:** Fuel 2–3 hours before with complex carbs (30–50 g) and protein (20 g) for sustained energy. Opt for simple carbs (honey, fruit, maple syrup, or even candy in a pinch) when time is short, as this will burn up very quickly when your sport begins.
   b. **Intra-Workout:** Sip electrolyte-rich drinks with 15–30 g of simple carbs per hour of intense exercise to maintain energy and prevent dehydration. Make sure the electrolytes are high in sodium and potassium to minimize cramping and fatigue.
   c. **Post-Workout:** Consume 25–30 g of protein and 60–90 g of carbs within 30 minutes of your training session to kickstart muscle repair and replenish glycogen stores. Chocolate milk provides the perfect ratio. Opt for lactose-free brands if lactose sensitive.
5. **Finding a Diet that Works for You:** Diets are short-term strategies to accomplish a specific goal. Finding what works for you, whether it's intermittent fasting, keto, or plant-based, will take some experimenting. Stick to the 80/20 principle at all times—80 percent of your food should come from whole food, and 20 percent of it can come from fun stuff. Manipulate your

Unit XI. Conclusion: Fueling Your Sport (cont.)

calories up and down, keeping track of macronutrients. Avoid fad diets, and supplement accordingly to make sure you aren't deficient in any of the macronutrients or micronutrients.

6. **Supplements as Tools:** Supplements should never make up the bulk of your diet. They are to supplement an already good diet and eating regimen. Once you've established what works for your body as far as your diet goes, then begin to add in supplements to increase your performance. Choose safe, evidenced-based supplements like whey protein, creatine, electrolytes, and multivitamins to help bridge your nutritional gaps. Always prioritize whole foods and consult with a physician before starting any supplement regimen.
7. **Micronutrients & Hydration:** Vitamins and minerals support immune function, energy production, and recovery. Eat a variety of whole foods (80/20 rule) to meet these needs. Replace electrolytes in warm weather or extreme periods of practice or training to prevent dehydration and keep your performance up while minimizing risks of injury.
8. **Body Composition for Sports-Specific Success:** Let me be clear, you should not focus on getting to a particular "body weight." Focus on an ideal body composition for your individual life and sport. Body composition reflects your body fat percentage and amount of lean muscle mass rather than just weight. Different sports require different compositions, and reaching these compositions will help maximize your athletic performance and help avoid eating disorders down the road.

Key Definitions

1. **Basal Metabolic Rate (BMR):** The calories your body burns at rest to maintain basic functions like breathing and circulation; the minimum amount of calories you need to stay alive
2. **Total Daily Energy Expenditure (TDEE):** The calories burned daily when including all of your normal activity; calculated as body weight (pounds) x activity factor (12–22 calories/pound)
3. **Calorie Deficit:** Consuming fewer calories than you burn through your TDEE, which leads to weight loss
4. **Calorie Surplus:** Consuming more calories than you burn through your TDEE, which leads to weight gain
5. **Macronutrients:** Protein, carbohydrates, and fats required in large amounts for energy, growth, repair, and hormone production
6. **Micronutrients:** Vitamins and minerals needed in small amounts for bodily functions like immune health, muscle contractions, bone strength, and hormone production
7. **Energy Systems:** Our body's three motors—the **ATP-PC** (creatine, 0–15 seconds of intense work), **glycolytic** or **anaerobic** (glucose, 15 seconds–2 minutes of intense work), and **oxidative** or **aerobic** (fat/glucose, anything more than 2 minutes of lower-intensity work)

Final Thoughts

As a teen athlete, you're at a pivotal stage in your growth and development where nutrition can not only shape your performance, but also shape your lifelong health. These fundamental nutrition skills will help with your athletic performance and carry over into your adult life, giving you the tools to fight off obesity and obesity-related diseases such as cardiovascular disease, stroke, cancer, Alzheimer's, autoimmune diseases, and frailty. Your body is capable of incredible feats, so fuel it wisely, listen to its signals, and build habits that will carry your athletic performance to higher and higher levels.

Answer Keys

Note: Answers for activities with definite answers are given below.

Activity 1: My Monthly Calorie Needs (p. 5)

Month	Calorie Range	My Daily Calorie Needs
Feb.	128 x 18–22 = 2,304–2,816	(2,304 + 2,816)/2 = ~2,560
Mar.	132 x 15–17 = 1,980–2,244	(1,980 + 2,244)/2 = ~2,112
Apr.		(1,596 + 1,862)/2 = ~1,729
May	135 x 15–17 = 2,025–2,295	(2,025 + 2,295)/2 = ~2,160
June	135 x 18–22 = 2,430–2,970	(2,430 + 2,970)/2 = ~2,700
July	137 x 18–22 = 2,466–3,014	(2,466 + 3,014)/2 = ~2,740
Aug.	138 x 15–17 = 2,070–2,346	(2,070 + 2,346)/2 = ~2,208
Sept.	136 x 12–14 = 1,632–1,904	(1,632 + 1,904)/2 = ~1,768
Oct.	138 x 15–17 = 2,070–2,346	(2,070 + 2,346)/2 = ~2,208
Nov.	141 x 15–17 = 2,115–2,397	(2,115 + 2,397)/2 = ~2,256

Activity 5: Vitamin Match-Up (p. 25)

1. vitamin D 2. vitamin K 3. vitamin B1
4. vitamin B3 5. vitamin B6 6. vitamin B9
7. vitamin B12 8. vitamin B7 9. vitamin B5
10. vitamin B2 11. vitamin C 12. vitamin E
13. vitamin A

Activity 6: Mineral Match-Up (p. 26)

1. chloride 2. manganese 3. phosphorus
4. copper 5. zinc 6. selenium
7. calcium 8. sulfur 9. magnesium
10. sodium 11. potassium 12. chromium
13. iron 14. iodine

Activity 8: Matching Body Fat Percentages (p. 36)

1. C 2. A 3. B 4. F 5. D 6. E

Activity 9: Figuring Body Fat Percentages (p. 36)

1. 20, 160, 12.5
2. 12, 125, 9.6
3. 12, 97, 12.4
4. 22, 143, 15.4
5. 30, 176, 17

Activity 11: Nutrition & Hydration Word Unscramble (p. 49)

1. PROTEIN 2. HYDRATION
3. MACRO 4. ELECTROLYTES
5. PRE-WORKOUT 6. CREATINE
7. POST-WORKOUT 8. CALORIE SURPLUS
9. FATS 10. AMINO ACIDS
11. SUPPLEMENTATION 12. CARBOHYDRATE
13. INTRA-WORKOUT 14. MICRO
15. CALORIE DEFICIT

Activity 13: Supplement Match-Up (p. 59)

Whey Protein—B—2
Creatine—A—3
Electrolytes—C—4
Multivitamin—D—1

Activity 14: Supplement Fill-in-the-Blank (p. 59)

1. cognition
2. Protein
3. Electrolytes
4. multivitamins
5. lactose
6. blood tests